Magic for Beginners
2

PRIMA PUBLISHING and its colophon, which consists of the letter P over PRIMA, are trademarks of Prima Communications, Inc.

Cover design by The Dunlavey Studio, Sacramento

Library of Congress Cataloging-in-Publication Data

Baron, Harry,
Magic for beginners 2 : card tricks and other close-up illusions / Harry Baron.
p.   cm.
Includes index.
ISBN 0-7615-0017-0
1. Conjuring. I. Title. II. Title: Magic for beginners two.
GV1547.B274 1995
793.8—dc20   95-3352

95 96 97 98 99 RRD 10 9 8 7 6 5 4 3 2 1
Printed in the United States of America

How to Order:
Single copies may be ordered from Prima Publishing, P.O. Box 1260BK, Rocklin, CA 95677; telephone (916) 632-4400. Quantity discounts are also available. On your letterhead, include information concerning the intended use of the books and the number of books you wish to purchase.

Magic for Beginners
2

Card Tricks and Other Close-Up Illusions

Harry Baron

PRIMA PUBLISHING

Contents

Introduction

MAGIC as a hobby is unique, because those who take it up enjoy a special thrill in being able to mystify their friends as well as entertain them. It is also unusual in that you can enjoy it even when alone: reading books on magic and practising the tricks can be most absorbing and, while doing so, you have the pleasurable anticipation of performing these same tricks later before small or large audiences.

Every trick in this book has been selected for its simplicity; in the main they make use of items that are easily found in the pocket or around the house, or, in the case of special props, that are easily carried. Many of the tricks can be worked absolutely impromptu with no preparation whatsoever, while others require only a little setting up. It all depends where and when you are going to perform. There are several effects, in fact, which are better performed when the audience is comfortably seated around you, but in general the emphasis of the book is on the 'right-under-your-nose' type.

You will discover as you read on that there are a number of tricks which can be adapted to even larger audiences, so while the book is not intended to be all-embracing, it undoubtedly contains material for everyone. Some effects are not conjuring tricks as such; many are little more than clever and amusing stunts or puzzles, but intriguing to the spectators none the less—certainly fun to do and watch.

With the know-how and only a little skill, plus a great deal of enthusiasm, you can really set out to have fun with magic and add a new dimension to your own and your friends' enjoyment.

CHAPTER ONE

Card Tricks

MISCALL

OUR first effect is a card trick; notice that we use the word 'effect', which means, in conjuring parlance, the impression or effect that is made upon the audience, and in this sense the word will be used constantly throughout the book.

In this case the spectators see the following: A pack of cards is given to someone to shuffle. Someone else is handed a pencil and paper and asked to write down the numbers from one to eight in a column. Any one of these numbers is now ringed round. The top eight cards are then counted off and handed to you. You call off the names of the cards one by one while they are written down against the numbers on the paper. Just initials will do: for instance, KD will stand for King of Diamonds, 4C will represent the four of Clubs and so on.

Someone now shuffles the eight cards into the pack. You ask the writer the name of the card against the number which was ringed round. Supposing it was the 9H (nine of Hearts); ask the spectator to look for that card in the pack and, to everyone's surprise, it cannot be found—it has completely vanished! You now direct someone's attention to a place behind the mirror and, wonder of wonders, the missing card is found there. This sounds an impossible feat of magic and, what is more, it requires no skill or practice. The cards are quite ordinary and you could have had no idea which number was going to be ringed round. It can even be done with a borrowed pack and quite impromptu, but more of that later.

No doubt you are wondering why this trick is titled Miscall; well, that is the basic secret, as you will learn very soon, but first of all, you must have the pencil and paper and the pack of cards handy. There is a little preparation necessary and it is simply this—before you show the trick, secretly remove any card from the pack and hide it anywhere, e.g. behind the mirror or under the carpet. Remember the name of the card; let us suppose it is the nine of Hearts.

Now you proceed just as previously described—hand the pack for shuffling—instruct someone to write down the column of figures and to ring any figure round. They have a perfect freedom of choice about this, of course, but you must note which figure it is; for example, it may be number four. Ask the person with the cards to deal the top eight face down onto your hand. Pick off the first card—look at it— call out its name; it might be the Ace of Clubs—the writer writes it against figure 1. The second card could be the three of Spades—you call three of Spades—he writes 3S against figure 2. The third card is called and each time you casually allow a glimpse of the card. Now the important subtlety takes place. When you come to the fourth card, you 'Miscall' it, that is to say, you do not announce its actual name, but instead call out the name of the card you concealed behind the mirror. This card is entered against figure 4. Do not allow the face of this card to be seen, but be casual about it. Carry on with the rest of the cards calling their names so they can be written down. Hand the cards to be shuffled into the pack and, from this point, you do not handle them.

You come now to the dramatic effect. Ask the writer which figure was ringed round (you already know it of course,

but appear to become interested in it only at this point).
Ask him to name the card written against the ringed figure,
then have the spectator look for it in the pack. He does not
find it and finally you produce it from your original
hiding place.

This excellent trick is capable of variations—for
instance, the whole sequence can be worked impromptu.
You borrow a pack, but as you remove the cards from the
case, secretly leave one behind; be sure to note which card
it is. You proceed exactly as before, but in this case the
missing card is found to have vanished from the pack, to
appear in the card case.

THE CARD ON THE CEILING

THERE is a certain hostelry in the City of London where, if
you happened to glance at the ceiling, you would no doubt
be intrigued by the presence of several playing cards stuck
there. It is a very high ceiling, too; if you enquire how they
came to be in this lofty position, the reply would be that
they were put there by a 'magician fellow'. No one seems to
know his exact identity for he is apparently an itinerant
performer, but he was prevailed upon from time to time to
perform this marvellous feat of causing a selected card to
appear on the ceiling.

How was it done? No one had a clue, but the cards
were left there permanently because it encouraged so much
comment. The identity of the mysterious conjuror still
remains as much an enigma, for he is long gone, but the
cards remain even though they have been varnished over to
preserve them. What is certain, however, is that this card
trick, successfully performed, is a real attention-getter and
people talk about it long after.

Very simply the effect is that a selected and signed

card is replaced in the pack which is then returned to its box. The box is thrown sharply against the ceiling and, as it falls away, the signed chosen card is left remaining on the ceiling in full view. This could truly be termed a classic effect, and like all classic effects (even though the secret of this one has been closely guarded) the method of accomplishment is extremely simple.

In this version the card is made to adhere to the ceiling by a band of clear cellulose sticky tape, rather like a cigar band with the sticky side outwards and just large enough to encircle the finger. Keep this in a small plastic pill-box until you are ready to use it (Fig. 1). Before you commence the trick, have it ready on the third finger of the left hand which is kept folded down into the palm. This should not restrict your handling of the cards too much.

The method of working is straightforward—just have the pack shuffled and fanned face up. Ask someone to point to any card. The fan is broken at this point—all the cards above their selected card are replaced underneath the pack. The selected card is now on top, face up. Holding the complete pack and using it as a desk, get the person to sign it. The signed card is now picked off with the right hand whilst the left hand turns the pack face down. Actually, what happens here is that *two* cards are lifted off as one (double-lift) and both are replaced on top of the pack as one (see p. 156). The spectators think the top card is their card. This is taken and placed somewhere in the centre of the deck. Casually turn the deck face up so the selected card comes against the sticky band which is pressed on the back of the card, and is removed from the finger by a sliding motion.

Square up the pack still face towards the spectators but, in doing so, allow the top (selected) card to protrude down from all the others by a small fraction. Replace the

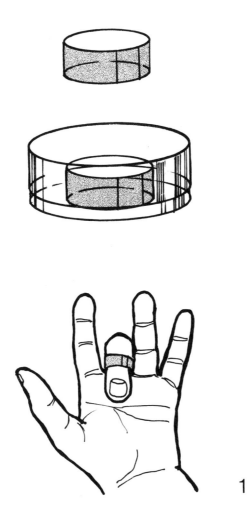

1

cards in the box, backs towards yourself. As you slide them in, allow the selected card to remain outside the box; this is made easy as it protrudes slightly at the bottom. (See Fig. 2 (your view).) Close the flap. Now throw the cards, complete in their case, squarely against the ceiling, so that the back card hits it firmly, where it will remain, whilst the case falls away to be deftly caught by you.

Naturally you must choose the time and, particularly, the location to work this spectacular stunt, but if done with a modicum of showmanship, it will prove to be a real stunner.

CALYPSO

AFTER the pack is shuffled it is handed to a spectator and the performer turns his back. The assistant is instructed to deal any number of cards, face down on the table. He stops at any point, notes the card stopped at, then replaces all the cards back on the pack. The pack is now cut several times. The performer turns round and endeavours to find the selected card, saying that he will 'take two chances', and lays two cards face down on the table.

The spectator is asked to select one of them and, on being turned over, it is seen to be the selected card. The performer now asks how many cards he counted to; when told he turns the second card and it is seen to represent this number. For instance, if he counted to eight cards, the card turned up will be an eight.

This particular trick can be very baffling to the onlooker, but does not require a great deal of skill to perform. The pack can be borrowed and there is no set-up necessary— it is almost a perfect card trick.

You begin by shuffling the pack and in doing so, note the bottom card, which is eventually shuffled to the top.

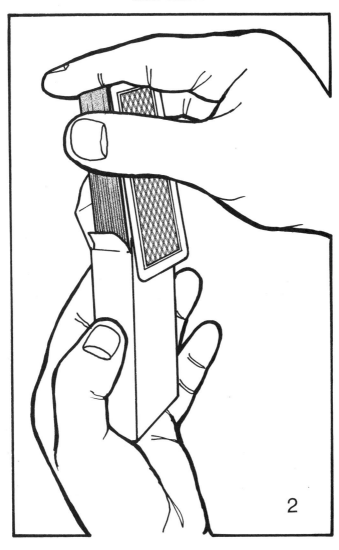

2

Hand the pack to someone to place face down on the table, but as you do so, remember which is now the bottom card. *You now know the top and bottom cards.* For example, they might be King of Diamonds at the top and Ace of Spades at the bottom. Turn your back and have your assistant deal the cards one at a time on the table. He can stop whenever he chooses, but he is to remember *how many he dealt.* When he stops, he is asked to pick up the *last card dealt,* remember it and replace it, face down, on the remainder of the pack. The dealt-off cards are squared up and placed on the pack also. The whole pack can now be cut several times. On receiving the pack, you turn the cards, faces to you, and run through them looking for the top card (King of Diamonds). When you find it, *the card immediately in front of it will be the selected card.* Remove it and place it face down on the table. Cut the King of Diamonds to the face of the pack. Now count all the cards behind the King of Diamonds until you reach the Ace of Spades, noting the number of cards *between* them—mentally add 2 to this number (for instance the amount of cards might total eight), and then take a card to a similar value, say eight of Hearts, and lay it face down beside the other. Whichever one is turned up first, it will reveal the card selected or the number dealt; turn up the second card and the trick is brought to a successful conclusion.

REVERSO

PERHAPS on reading this you might think the trick would not be effective, but try it and see; it's incredibly simple, but it has a surprising result.

Openly remove the four Aces from the pack and hand them to someone to arrange in any order he likes. While this is being done it will give you the opportunity unobtrusively to reverse the bottom card of the pack.

Turn the pack over so that all the cards are now face down except the top card—but the audience should not suspect this. You now take the Aces one by one and place them in the pack in different places. Be careful not to reveal the cards are not really face down. Placing the cards behind your back, tell your audience you are going to try and locate the Aces. All you have to do behind your back is to reverse the top face-down card and turn the pack over. Then bring the cards from behind your back and spread them on the table. It will now be seen that you have reversed the four Aces in the pack.

QUICK FOUR ACE

THIS is a very rapid four-Ace trick and looks far more clever than it really is. Remove the four Aces from the pack and place three other cards on your left hand, face up. Put the four Aces on top of these three cards, also face up. You now spread the Aces so that the three cards are concealed behind the first Ace.

Now you are ready to perform. Display the cards in a fan as if there were only four Aces there. Put them face down on top of the pack. Now deal the top four cards out in a row face down, from right to left. Unknown to the spectators, only one (the first on the left) is an Ace. Deal the next three cards onto this (they are all Aces, but the spectators think they are ordinary cards). Follow up by dealing three cards on each of the other three piles.

Gather all the piles up from right to left, placing them on top of the pack (Ace pile goes on top). Give the cards a flick, turn over the top four cards and they are all seen to be Aces. Remember to do this at a rapid rate explaining as you do so.

CARD SURPRISE

REMOVE the four Aces and any King from the pack, place the King face up on the bottom, then put the four Aces face down beneath the King. Square up the pack and you are all ready to present a surprising little card trick requiring absolutely no skill. Fan the cards and have one selected. (The only thing you *must not* do is reveal that there is a face-up card near the bottom.)

The selected card is noted and placed on top of the pack and the spectator is asked to cut the deck and complete the cut. Say that you will now cause his selected card to turn over in the pack. Keeping the cards still face down, go to the King. Of course, he will say this is not the selected card, so place all the cards *above* the King on the bottom of the pack. Then lay the King face up on the table and spell the word K I N G—one card for each letter, laying the next four cards *face down* in a row beside the face-up King. Ask the name of the card, turning the next one face up, and to the spectator's surprise, it will be *his selected card*. But here's the punch—you say, 'Well, here's the King, and here's your card and, strangely enough, these cards are *all the Aces*.' (Turn up the four face-down cards as you say this to show they are the four Aces.)

SPELL IT

TAKE one of the suits out of a pack of playing cards, Clubs, Hearts or whichever is your favourite suit. Arrange it in the following order, 3-8-7-Ace-Queen-6-4-2-Jack-King-10-9-5, reading from left to right, face up. Replace this set-up suit face down on top of your face-down pack and you are ready to work an interesting card cameo.

First of all, give the pack a riffle shuffle which distributes your set-up suit (let's say Clubs) throughout the pack, but keeping it in the same order.

Now turn the cards face up; tell your audience you will take the Club suit out of the pack. Run through the cards and, each time you come to a Club, take it out of the pack and place it face down on the table. This will leave the cards in the same order you had originally on top of the pack. Pick up the set-up cards, hold them face down in your hand (three at the top and five at the bottom), spell out A C E by putting one card from the top of the pack to the bottom for each letter; turn up the fourth card—it will be the Ace. Throw the Ace on the table; again put one card at a time from the top to the bottom of the pack, spell T W O, turn up the next card, and it will be the two. Throw the two on the table and continue in the same manner until you have spelt out correctly each of the other cards, finishing up with the King which is left in your hand.

CHAPTER TWO

Stunts

TOUGH GLASS

D O you think you can bend a coin with a glass tumbler? It can be done! Select a strong straight-sided glass and place a coin on the table; begin tapping it with the base of the glass. You must hold the glass as shown in Fig. 3. The

coin is sharply rapped with the edge of the thick base. After repeated blows in the same spot, the coin will begin to bend upwards (Fig. 4). Naturally it is not advisable to use the best table for the effect and it does make rather a lot of noise, so select the right time to put this stunt over. Fig. 5 shows what the end product looks like.

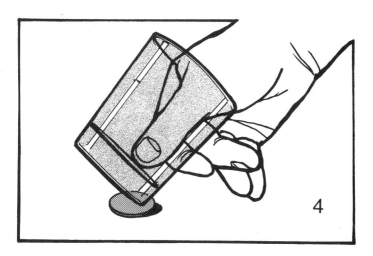

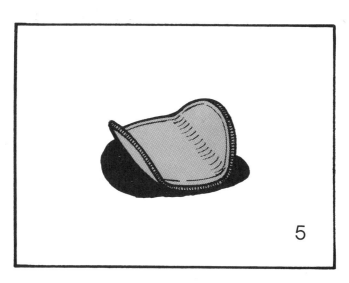

WACKY WINE GLASS

Effect The magician picks up any wine glass and casually unscrews the base which is immediately tossed into the air. It is deftly caught and then screwed back on again. The glass is returned to the table none the worse for its ordeal.

This is an apparently impromptu stunt but none the less quite effective and very amusing if carried out briskly. You will need to wait until an 'accident' happens to a wine glass, and as this seems to occur fairly frequently you will soon have the necessary prop which will last you for many performances. Break off the base as near to the bottom of the stem as you can. Smooth off the small remaining piece of stem with abrasive paper. This gimmick is seen in Fig. 6.

Place this gimmick in your pocket and wait for a suitable occasion on which to perform the stunt, which incidentally should appear as if done on the spur of the moment.

Secure the gimmick and hold it concealed in the right hand. Pick up an empty wine glass with your left hand. Hold it as shown in Fig. 7 (your view). Note that the hand is face down with the fingers around the stem, the base pointing to the right. The right hand, which conceals the gimmick, approaches the bottom of the glass and you proceed apparently to unscrew it with a few twisting movements (Fig. 8). Toss the gimmick into the air, following it with your eyes and covering the real base with the left fingers. Catch the gimmick with the right hand (Fig. 9), display it for the briefest moment and immediately proceed to appear to screw it back on again. Don't worry about any clicking noise you make, it will enhance the effect. Show the glass, palming the gimmick with the right hand, and as you replace the glass on the table, drop the gimmick back into

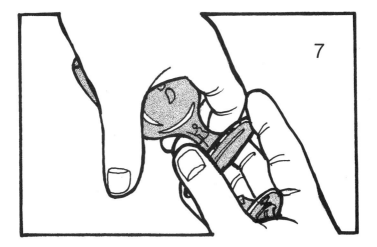

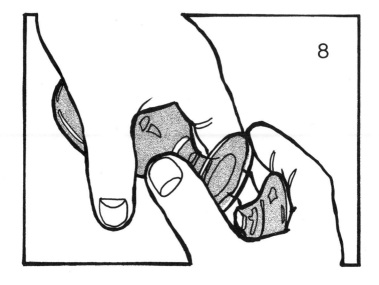

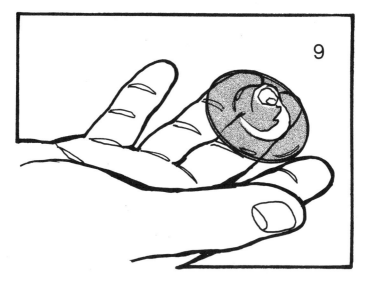

your right pocket. Remember, the whole operation depends on surprise and must be executed briskly and with great aplomb. It is more amusing than mystifying but very effective.

VANISHING GLASS

THE effect is adapted from a similar stunt by the Rigoletto Brothers whom I saw perform it using a huge crystal ball. This was over thirty years ago at the old Magician's Club, London.

Effect The magician stands in a group of friends and requests the loan of a handkerchief, which he drapes over a small glass. Several people are invited to reach under the hanky to feel if the glass is actually there. Suddenly, the hanky is pulled through the fist and tossed in the air . . . the glass has completely vanished.

Secret This requires a little audacity to work, but it has an unbelievably dramatic effect on the audience. You can even have liquid in the glass and that disappears as well! Actually, an accomplice is used to help you achieve the trick.

Working Borrow the handkerchief and, picking up a small glass, drape it over the top as shown in Fig. 10. Cup the fingers around the rim to simulate the shape of the glass as in the sketch; you will notice the glass is in reality held just below the curled fingers. Go round to several people and invite them to feel *under* the hanky and touch the glass. They all verify that the glass is really there.

Go to your confederate friend last and ask him to feel the glass as the others did. Instead of merely feeling it,

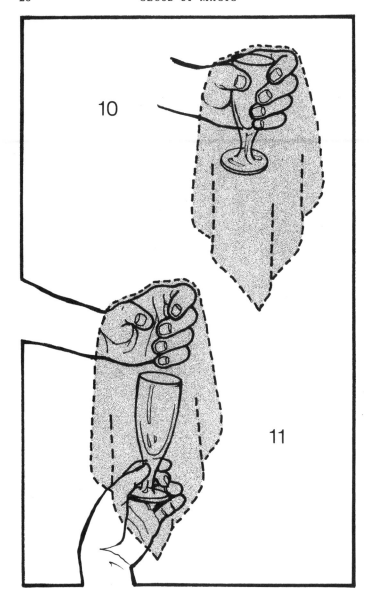

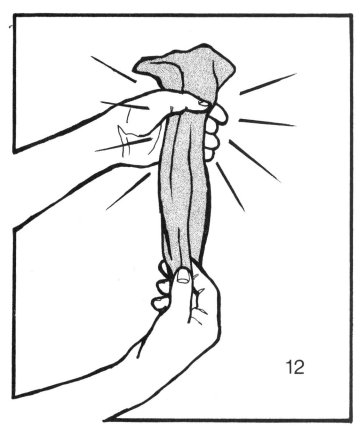

12

he actually takes hold of it, and as he does so, you move across in front of him in readiness for the vanish (Fig. 11). Your hand still retains the shape of the glass beneath the hanky. All attention is on you or rather the hanky, and this effectively covers your friend while he quietly and *un-hurriedly* deposits the glass on the table or bar. If most of the other people are also holding a drink, he may well retain the glass in his hand, as if it were his own. Meanwhile you are drawing attention to the glass under the hanky, saying 'Did you feel the glass under the handkerchief? Well, now it has gone!' Draw the hanky through the fist as in Fig. 12, then toss it into the air to show the glass has vanished.

Incidentally this effect has been worked on numerous occasions where even the stooge was, up to that point, unaware that he was going to help. I simply dump the glass in his hand and carry on; you will find that he will enjoy suddenly being let in on a secret. Choose a person who is alert, of course, and preferably standing close to the bar, so that it makes it easy for him to dispose of it.

Of course, the ideal presentation would be to have even a second stooge who knows what you are going to do; after the glass has actually been taken by the first, go to the second stooge who feels beneath the hanky and assures you that he can feel the glass as did the others. Without more ado, you can make the vanish really startling.

One disconcerting thing about this trick is that, on many an occasion, I have had the barman ask for his glass back, because he is certain that you have concealed it somewhere. It is not easy to convince him that it is usually there on his own bar staring him in the face.

DENTED CAN

ANOTHER interesting stunt, not really magic of course, but it is one of those items which people talk about afterwards.

Effect The performer takes an unopened can of beans, soup or almost anything that is in a sealed tin. Laying his thumb or finger on the table or floor, he immediately surprises everyone by crashing the can down with a sickening thud onto it. The can is seen to be well and truly dented, but no harm has apparently come to the finger. This feat can be repeated, but offers for other people to try it are usually rejected. It just takes a little courage plus the know-how to do it the first time.

In actual fact the wall of a tin can is quite soft and the middle part can be pressed in quite easily. It is the rims that really protect the thumb from damage. But make sure that the thumb is laid on a *solid* surface. Bring the can down smartly onto the thumb with a resounding thump, but hit the thumb centrally with the can—the wall of the can will cave in, and the two outside rims will protect the thumb. Avoid letting the seam, which is the toughest part of the wall, touch your thumb.

Fig. 13 shows how the can is held in the right hand. Fig. 14 shows the can almost at the point of impact, while the drawing (Fig. 15) depicts the point of impact as well as indicating the seam of the can on top (here the finger is used—see which you find easier). Fig. 16 shows you what the can looks like after impact—it is really quite an impressive stunt.

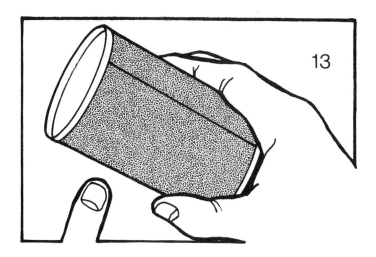

13

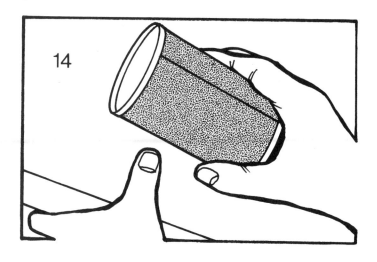

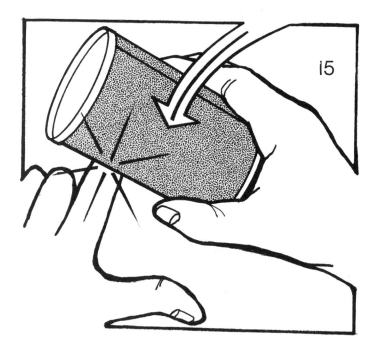

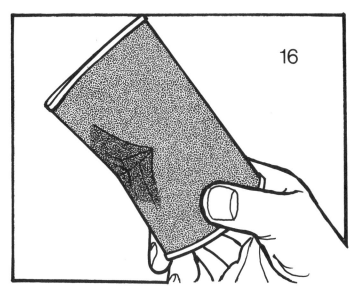

Two or three dents can be made in one can, all at different places of course; after this you can let someone else have a try, and if they use the same can they will not be so lucky. Avoid using cans of beer or Coke in case they have to be opened soon. The banging about will have a disturbing effect on the contents, but the *trick* will still work, nevertheless. This should be performed under the supervision of an adult.

SUPER-NORMAL STRENGTH

THIS is an impromptu stunt which the performer can put over at parties, etc. It is quite a talking point and is very mystifying to those who do not know the secret. In fact, this secret is little known and it is advisable to keep it to yourself, because the knowledge of this effect will gain you quite a reputation over the years.

The only prop needed is a strong staff of wood—a broom-stick is ideal. The effect is that the performer is able easily to hold the staff while the full force of several strong people push against it.

The staff is held horizontally at about chest height and is gripped with the hands, backs uppermost and about 18 inches apart. Now three or four people take up position directly opposite you and take a firm grip on the staff. They are instructed not to begin until you say so and then they are all to press concertedly and *steadily* (not jerkily) against *your* pressure on the staff, from the opposite direction. *The secret is simply a matter of deflecting their force in an upward direction.*

It is important that they push against the staff steadily and, as they do, you *steadily* exert an *upward* and *forward* pressure. You will then find that you will easily be able to resist the full force of their combined efforts. Try it, it really works, but confidence is the keynote.

IT'S A KNOCK OUT

DURING a lull in a game of draughts, show this rather amazing feat.

Take several white draughts and one black one. Form them in a stack with the black one second from the bottom. The problem is to remove the black one from the stack without touching them and without causing the stack to tumble over.

Here's how: Take another draught and stand it on edge a few inches away from the stack. Press down on this draught with your forefinger as shown in Fig. 17 until it is propelled forwards towards the stack. (See sketch.) When it hits the pile of draughts, the black one will flip out, leaving the rest of the stack undisturbed.

A PINCH OF SMOKE

REACHING into a puff of cigarette smoke, you appear to take a 'pinch' of it between your thumb and finger.

The audience will be mildly amused by this little pantomime, but watch their faces when little puffs of smoke actually begin to emit from your fingers.

Your hand can be examined thoroughly and the spectators will be none the wiser.

You will require a match-box, the type having a *brown* striking surface; no other will do.

Carefully peel away a very thin layer of the brown striking surface and placing it in a receptacle such as a large spoon, set light to it. After it has burned away, you will notice that a brown, gum-like residue will remain.

This is the magic stuff to make the mysterious smoke. By simply rubbing it gently between the finger and thumb you will produce the smoke as if from thin air. Please wash your hands thoroughly afterwards.

CHAPTER THREE

Mental Effects

IMPROMPTU BOOK TEST

ADD up all the figures on a bank note, e.g. 62N551790 (which in this instance comes to 35). Crumple the note into a ball and place it handy in your pocket. Secretly glimpse the fifth word on the third line on page 35 in a book already in the room.

Borrow a similar note and as soon as it is handed to · you crumple it into a ball and switch it for your own. This is easily accomplished by having your own note held loosely against the curled fingers in your right hand. Under cover of the crumpling motion, contrive to twist the position of the two notes, eventually bringing your one to view. This is handed to someone to place on top of the book. If you can use the 'Conjuror's Choice' to have it 'selected' from several, so much the better.

Now ask a person to open the note and to add all the numbers together. He is instructed to turn to the appropriate page in the book—count down the line and along it to arrive at the word. He is asked to remember it and close the book. You now reveal the word in any way you desire.

NB The 'Conjuror's Choice' principle is fully described in 'Who'll Buy the Drinks?' on p. 83.

NEWSPAPER PREDICTION

THE performer first writes a prediction and places it to one side. Then, taking a newspaper, he cuts from it with scissors a complete column of print. The rest of the paper is discarded and the strip of paper is held at the finger tips as the scissors are slowly passed from top to bottom. A spectator calls 'stop' at any time and, at this precise spot, the column is snipped in two. A spectator now reads the line at the point of cutting—the prediction is then read out and seen to be exact in every particular. A very subtle and delightfully simple method is employed and it can be done virtually impromptu.

The newspaper is quite ordinary, but you will need to pick a long column of print, preferably with no headline or other matter to break it up. Cut it from the paper, but start a line or two from the top. *This is the line you write as your prediction* (Fig. 18). Now, holding the strip at the top between finger and thumb, slowly move the scissors down until someone calls stop. Cut the paper in two at this point (Figs. 19, 20 and 21).

The subtlety employed here is that the column of paper is held *upside down*. This is unsuspected by the audience because they are a few feet away. Cut when they say so, allowing the lower part to flutter to the floor, where it is picked up by a spectator. While it is still in his hands, he reads the line; naturally he reads your original top line, the one you have already predicted.

Fig. 22 shows the two pieces of paper after being cut. The strip was originally held at A and cut at B. Part X is retained in the hand while part Y is allowed to flutter to the floor where it is retrieved by the spectator. When asked to read the top line he naturally reads off the original top line of the column, the one you have predicted and shown ringed round in Fig. 22.

A simple trick, requiring a minimum of props.

The top line in this particular case reads 'perhaps at his best' so this is the prediction you make.

18

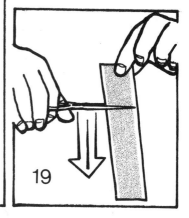

19

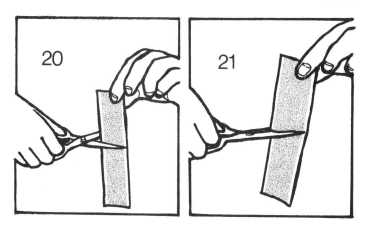

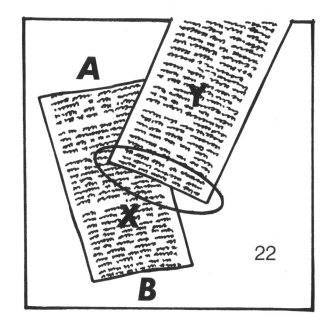

MIND BENDER

HERE is an interesting stunt to carry around in the wallet. Copy out the figures on a piece of card as shown in Fig. 23. When showing it to a friend, begin by covering up all but the top line and ask him to call out the figure. Move the hand down to reveal the second line, telling him to add them together; move down to the third line, adding this figure and so on down to the bottom. Still keep the total covered. It's surprising how many people will make the total 5,000. Try it yourself and see!

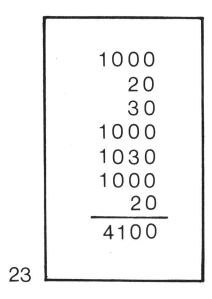

23

COUNT DOWN

YOU will need fifty small tiddley-wink chips or counters. They are easily obtainable from a games and toy shop. Twenty-five should be of one colour, say red, the other twenty-five possibly blue, but any two colours will do.

The fifty chips are put in a box or hat and thoroughly mixed. While this is being done, you make a prediction on a piece of paper and place it to one side for a moment. Now ask one of the audience to take out the chips at random *two* at a time. If they both happen to be blue, have them put in a pile on the left. If both of the next pair are blue, these are placed with them. If both of the next pair are red, they are placed in a pile on the right. If the next pair happens to be one of each colour they are placed in a pile in the centre. This goes on until all the chips are used up.

Now a rather intriguing thing here is that both the piles containing the like colours will always contain *an equal number of chips*. So you could make a straightforward prediction to this effect. For example, 'Both piles of the same colour will be equal in number.' But supposing you wish to repeat the effect, you can make the result come differently by secretly removing, say, four of the red chips. Your prediction can now read 'The blue pile will have four more chips in it than the red.'

If at the beginning you ask them to select a colour, you can write on the piece of paper, 'Your colour will have four more chips in it than the other' (or vice versa according to whichever colour is selected). Any number of chips can be secretly secured of course—it is this number which will affect the final result.

NB   As you read this you will probably not have the necessary chips to hand, so try it out using playing cards, i.e. 25 Black cards (Clubs and Spades) and 25 Red cards (Diamonds and Hearts).

LIVING AND DEAD

SEVERAL people are each handed a plain visiting card together with a pencil. They are asked secretly to write the name of a living person on their card—except for one person, who is told to write the name of a *dead* person. These are all dropped into a hat and mixed. No one except the person who wrote it knows the 'dead' name. However, taking up each card one at a time and by receiving 'thought vibrations' you are able to divine which one it is.

This effect depends more on the way it is presented than on the method, which is very simple indeed. All those asked to write a 'live' name are given a hard pencil and the person who is told to write the 'dead' name is given a soft pencil. The pencils all look alike of course. When you pick up the cards one by one, you are easily able to detect the one written in soft lead.

CHAPTER FOUR

Pins, Rope and String

INDESTRUCTIBLE STRING

A PIECE of string is threaded through a straw and both are cut through the centre—the straw falls away in two parts, but the string remains undamaged.

The secret lies in the straw which has had a fine slit cut in it at about the centre (X) (Fig. 24). First thread the

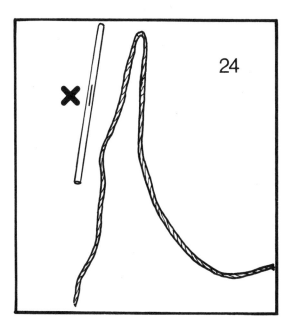

24

string through the straw, then fold the straw in half, the slit being underneath. Pull down very slightly on the ends of the string in order to pull it through the slit (Fig. 25). Insert the point of the scissors *above* the string and cut through the straw. The spectators think the string is being cut also, but when the two halves of the straw are drawn apart, the string is of course undamaged.

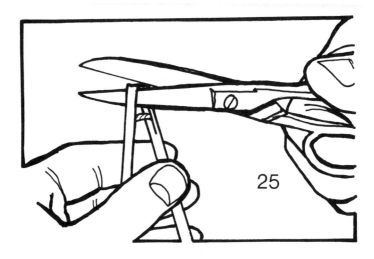

25

HAMBURG ROPE TRICK

ONE of the most popular magic feats among conjurors is the rope cutting trick where, after the rope is cut into pieces, it is restored whole again. There are countless methods and some are better than others; the Hamburg Rope Trick is one of the best.

It has the advantage that the rope is completely unprepared—in fact it can be performed with a piece of borrowed string and done impromptu if desired; it is also perfect as a stage effect if you use the soft white cotton rope

available from magic dealers. You will require a piece about
5 or 6 feet long and also a pair of sharp scissors.

This particular version, which I have used for many
years, makes use of a most ingenious move invented by
Edward Victor and is undoubtedly the most deceptive ever.
Coupled with the principle of the 'Panama Rope Trick',
devised by Ted Collins of America, it is just about perfect.
It has been marketed for many years under the above title.

The first move is apparently to pick up the centre of
the rope, forming it into a loop in the left hand, and then
cutting through it, seemingly cutting the rope into two
pieces. This is achieved by a series of moves which, although
lengthy to describe, takes only a second to do. In fact you
cut off only the extreme end of the rope which is left doubled
round the real centre looking as though the rope is cut in two.

(1) Hold the rope at one end (the other hanging down) in
the left hand, with about 2 inches of rope protruding above
the left fingers, the back of the hand towards the spectators.

(2) Place your right hand palm upwards under the centre
of the rope.

(3) Lift up the centre of the rope with this hand and bring
it towards the left hand, turning the right palm to the left
and towards you as you do so (Fig. 26).

(4) Note that the right thumb is put under the rope as it
nears the left hand.

(5) The right forefinger and thumb grasp the rope at a point
immediately under the left thumb (Fig. 27).

(6) Allow the centre point of the rope which is still lying
over the back of the right fingers to fall against the rope
held between the two thumbs.

(7) The right thumb and forefinger now bring up the bight
of the rope which they are now holding and level the loop
with the end in the left hand.

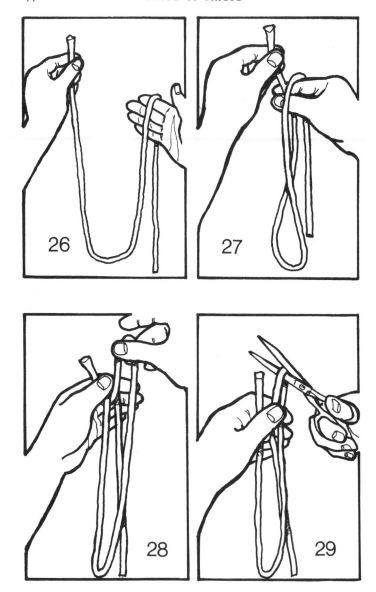

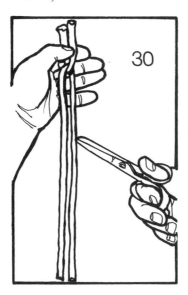

(8) Now the left thumb and forefinger grip the rope tightly at the point where the actual end passes under the real centre of the rope (Fig. 28).

(9) The rope is then cut through at the top of the visible loop (Fig. 29) and the long end allowed to drop down. The left hand appears to be holding two long pieces (Fig. 30).

(10) Tie the small piece around the large piece as if tying two long ropes together at the end, but do a double twist around the main rope before completing the knot. This gives a better appearance of a genuine knot.

(11) The next stage uses Ted Collins' subtlety. Take one end of the rope and tie it using a reef or square knot at a point midway between the Victor knot and the end. Study the drawings to see how this is done (Figs. 31, 32 and 33).

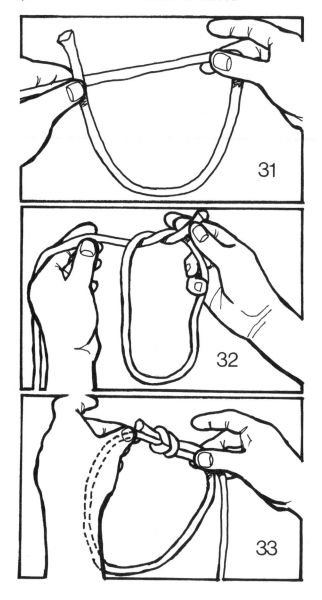

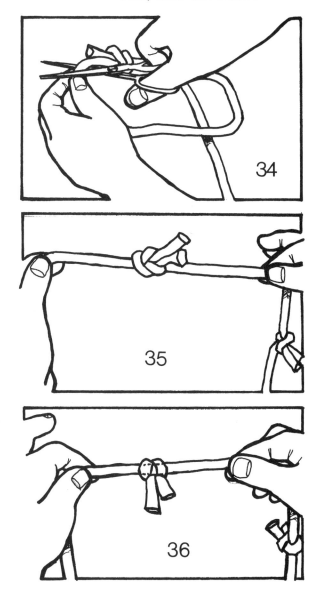

(12) Tie a similar loop in the opposite end of the rope.
(13) Now cut the two loops at a point opposite the short end of the rope as shown in Fig. 34. You will now have what appear to be four pieces of rope tied together at their ends. Pull the rope on either sides of the knots (Fig. 35)—this has the effect of straightening out the knot. All the knots are now, so to speak, 'sliding' knots and appear as in Fig. 36.

To bring the trick to its climax, take hold of one end of the rope and commence to wrap it round the left hand. When the right hand comes to the first knot, apply enough pressure on it to cause it to slide along the rope, the right fingers concealing it—however, appear to place the knot in the left hand as you continue to wrap the rope round it. Continue winding until the centre knot is reached—treating this and the last knot the same. Carry all the knots along the rope with the right hand until you reach the end where they come off into that hand unknown to the audience. Turn, with the left side to the spectators and, as you do so, raise your left hand allowing the rope to unwind, to reveal that it is now restored in one piece. While all attention is on this, quietly drop the loose knots into your right coat pocket. Turn to the front, pick up the other end of the rope with the right hand and pull it to prove that restoration is complete— then, if you wish, toss the rope out into the audience for examination.

UNLINKING PINS

Two large safety-pins are all that is required. They are linked together and, simply by giving them a sharp pull, the performer causes them to penetrate each other and come apart. This is done in three different ways in order to add confusion in the spectator's mind. Just a little practice is necessary to accomplish the 'release' effectively.

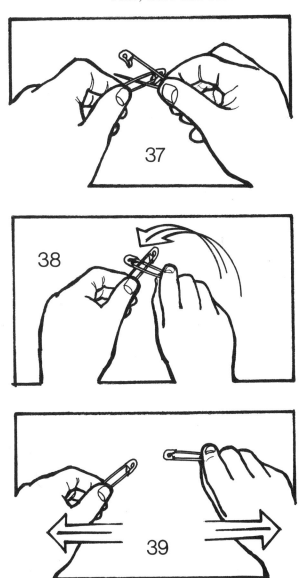

First release Hold a safety-pin by the hinge end between the thumb and forefinger of each hand. The pin in the right hand should be *open* and held so that the loose bar is at the bottom with the point to the left. The left-hand pin is *closed* and held with the fixed bar uppermost and with the point towards the right. Insert the point of the right-hand pin *down* through the left-hand pin and fasten. Fig. 37 should make this quite clear.

After closing the pin continue to hold them as in the drawing. Now turn the top pin sideways by simply twisting the right hand to the left. The pins should now appear as in Fig. 38. With a brisk sliding motion pull the pins apart; they will separate but still remain closed as in Fig. 39. A little practice will soon produce the knack of separating the pins smoothly.

Second release This is achieved in much the same way as the first but in this case the left-hand pin is held by its head with the hinge end pointing towards the right. Right-hand pin is held as before, loose bar downwards, point towards the left. Insert it into the left-hand pin and close. See Fig. 40. Turn the right-hand pin over to the left as before (Fig. 41). Pull the pins from each other to separate them and they will still remain closed.

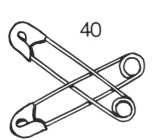

40

41

Third release On this occasion the pins are not actually linked together at all but, owing to the two previous methods, this subtlety is never suspected by the audience. One of the pins is unfastened and the pretence is gone through of linking the two pins together as before. In reality the point is passed *under* and not through the other pin. The open pin is closed and the two are held in a 'tail-to-tail' (Fig. 42) position with the forefinger and thumb, which conceal the actual points at which the two pins cross. The hands are then separated as before. Now both pins can immediately be passed for inspection.

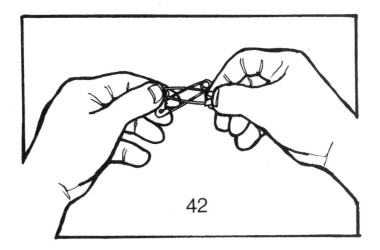

42

SAFETY RIP

THIS is a very good 'follow-up' to the preceding trick and makes use of one of the pins just used.

A person is asked to hold one corner of his handkerchief while you hold the other. You push a safety-pin through the hem, locking it in position. With a sudden movement the pin is 'ripped' along the hem. Everyone expects to see the hanky torn but, to their amazement, it remains undamaged.

Borrow the hanky and have the spectator hold one corner and, while facing him, you hold the other with the left hand so that it hangs down between you. The hanky must be held securely and stretched tightly at all times. Insert the pin with your right hand at a point near the left side of the hanky and fasten it as shown in Fig. 43. The hand is now turned over to the left, the pin also being turned sideways as in Fig. 44. The pin is drawn firmly and sharply to the right along the hanky towards the right-hand edge (Fig. 45) where it is again thrust through the cloth away from you; it locks in position once more.

Fig. 46 shows the pin being pushed through at the end of its 'run'. A little practice is required to perform this action neatly and it is suggested that you try it on some old cloth first.

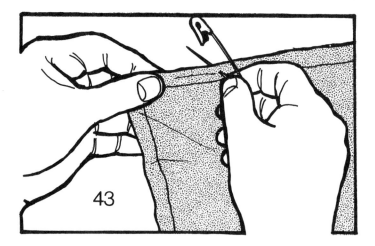

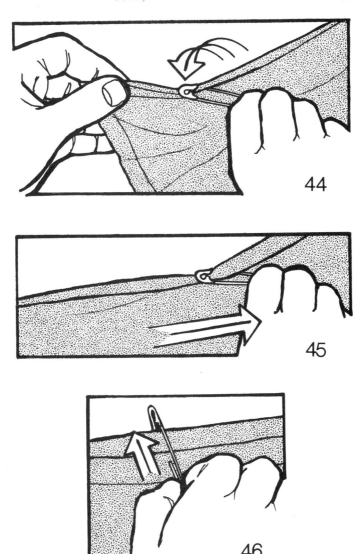

44

45

46

CHAPTER FIVE

Puzzles

THE RING AND THE SPRING

THIS is really a puzzle, but one that is so simple in effect and execution that it makes a worthwhile item to include in this book. In fact the victims in trying to puzzle it out think that trickery is involved.

A small ring and a spring are displayed and the performer simply drops the ring on the spring and immediately passes it to a spectator. To his surprise, he is unable to separate the ring from the spring.

Both the ring and spring are quite ordinary—the ring in fact could be a borrowed finger ring; the spring should be a short strong one as seen in Fig. 47.

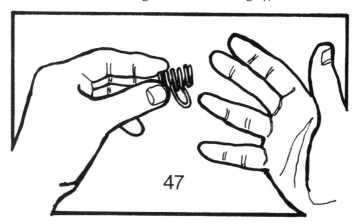

47

Hold the end of the spring between the finger and thumb of the left hand. Place the ring over the opposite end, bringing it to about the middle. Immediately hand it to the spectator, but as you do so secretly twist the ring to the right (as if turning a key). This has the effect of locking the ring onto the spring, and the only way to get it off is to twist it back again. The spectator will endeavour to get it off by turning the ring over the end of the spring, but this has the effect of only locking it onto two turns of the spiral instead of one (Fig. 48). Look around for the right type of spring and you will have a simple but 'puzzling' puzzle which will virtually last for ever.

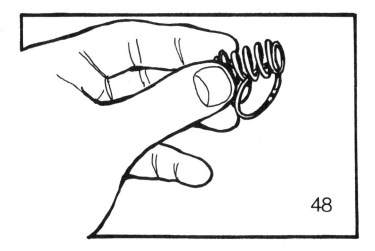

48

'KNOT' BY TUBE

YOU will require a tube made of plastic, metal or cardboard, about 3 inches long by $\frac{3}{4}$ inch in diameter, and a 2-foot length of cord. A knot is simply tied round the tube and one end threaded through it and the knot slipped off. Someone holds both ends of the cord. The problem is, 'Where is the knot—is it in the tube or in your hand?' The answer is surprising because each time it can be different. First the knot is in the tube, then in the hand, and finally it vanishes altogether!

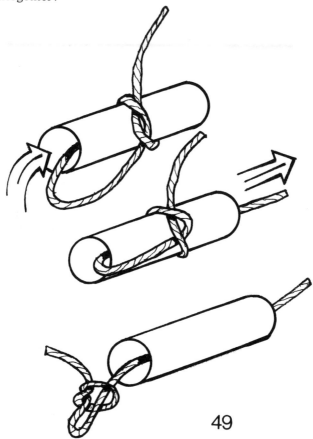

49

It all depends on which end of the rope and into which end of the tube you push it through to cause the knot to appear or vanish. Experiment and see, but in the sketch (Fig. 49) accompanying, you will see how the knot is made to vanish.

THE CREEPER

PLACE two piles of two coins on the tablecloth and put another single coin between them. Turn a glass tumbler upside down, resting the rim on the piles of coins as shown in Fig. 50. The problem is to take out the centre coin without touching the coins or the glass.

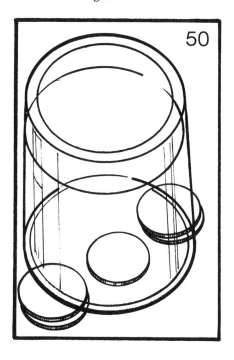

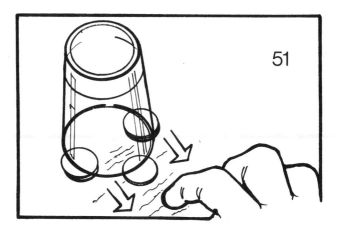

Simply scratch the tablecloth at a point just outside the glass (see arrow Fig. 51) and the captive coin will slowly 'creep' out.

TOPSY TUMBLERS

PLACE three glass tumblers on the table as shown in Fig. 52. Note the two outside ones are bottom up. Say that you are going to turn two glasses at a time in three turns, so they are all the right way up.

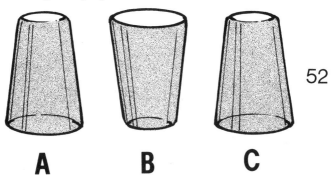

A   **B**   **C**

(1) Turn over A and B together.

(2) Turn over A and C together.

(3) Turn over A and B together.

Now turn over the centre glass and challenge your friend to do it. He will fail unless he twigs that, when you started, you had the centre one *upwards*, but you always try to let him start with the centre one downwards, because then it is impossible.

PUZZLELOOP

THIS is quite a puzzling novelty and causes much amusement. It is very simply made, as you will see from Fig. 53. A small stick, dowel or pencil is drilled at one end and a piece of twine is passed through the hole. This is knotted to form a loop such that, when extended, it will not be able to pass round the opposite end of the stick.

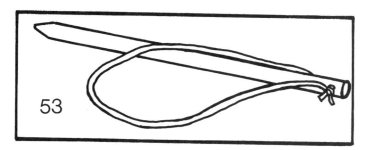

The effect is to fix the Puzzleloop through your victim's button-hole and challenge him to remove it without cutting the string or breaking the stick.

To put the Puzzleloop on: Pass your fingers and thumb through the loop and over the button-hole, pulling as much of the coat through the loop as possible. Now you will find that you are able to thread the stick through the button-hole quite easily (see Figs. 54 and 55). Draw the loop up tight as in Fig. 56.

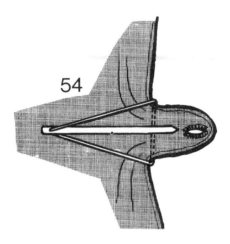

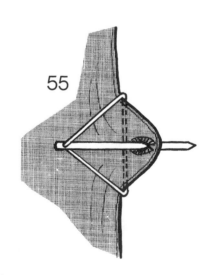

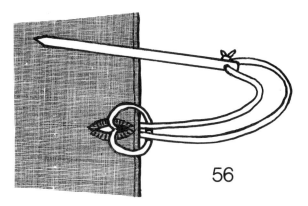

56

To remove the Puzzleloop: Reverse the above movements and, by again pulling the coat through the loop, you will find it comes off quite easily.

CHAPTER SIX

Money and Coin Tricks

SHRINKING MONEY

YOU do not need to be a magician these days in order to make your money shrink, but here is a way to prove that a pound note can shrink to half its size.

Borrow a paper note, telling your audience that you will now make it shrink to half its size. Roll it into a ball between your two palms. Continue rolling and rubbing the ball vigorously. After a while, open it out and spread it alongside another note to check for size. You will notice that the money is now appreciably smaller. Repeat the procedure and the note becomes smaller still. More of this same treatment will render the note almost unrecognizable. Incidentally, the lender will be quite horrified when you return his money to him. However, it is a good idea to have another note to give him in place of it. Later you can bring the note back to normal (albeit a little the worse for wear). This is done by carefully dampening the note and ironing all the creases out. Fig. 57 shows you what the note looks like after subjecting it to the 'shrinking' treatment.

FADE-AWAY COIN

A BORROWED coin virtually fades away even though it is held up to the last second by a spectator.

In a seated position, the performer folds the coin in the loose trouser material at a point just above the knee, where it is briefly held by the spectator. The coin, although

hidden, can be felt through the folds of the cloth. It is now taken by the performer and a rubbing motion seems to dissolve the coin away, the hands being shown unmistakably empty.

You will require a special fake for this trick, but it is easily made by drilling a small hole near the edge of a coin; or you could use a metal washer about the same size as a coin. A thin piece of twine or fishing line is attached to the coin. The other end of the line is tied to a safety-pin and the pin in turn is secured to a position *inside* the trousers so that it hangs down to a point just above the knee. Ascertain the length of line by trial. The working is comparatively simple.

When the coin has been borrowed it is apparently wrapped in the fold of the material, but in actual fact the thumb moves it aside so that the hidden coin *under* the cloth is wrapped instead.

The spectator is asked to grip the coin; under this misdirection and cover you are able to steal the original coin away and quietly deposit it in the pocket. Your hands empty, you take the still folded-down coin from the spectator and, with a 'crumbling' motion, 'dissolve' the coin away.

Of course, if you so wish you could have the original coin marked at the outset and eventually have it discovered inside a bun or a ball of wool. (On page 66 you will find an excellent routine where a coin vanishes and is later found inside a nest of purses.)

STAPLED COIN

A BORROWED and marked coin is folded in a square of paper and securely sealed by stapling together the four sides of the paper. Despite this, the coin vanishes, to reappear in a totally different place.

Use a piece of stiff paper about 3 inches by 2—you will also require a small pocket stapler.

The paper is previously prepared by putting a staple in the centre at one end (see Fig. 58 A). This is unknown to the audience—when handling it, conceal the staple with the left finger and thumb. The paper is creased down the centre and the marked coin is placed on the left of the crease (B). The right-hand part of the paper is now folded down over the coin and pressed down around it so that the outline of

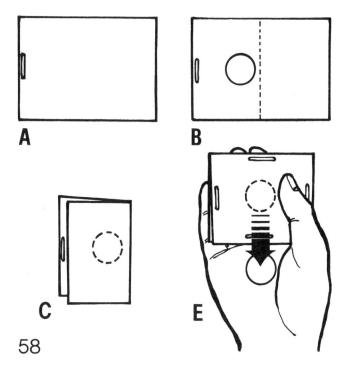

A

B

C

E

58

the coin is impressed on it (C). The bottom part, nearest you, is now stapled together. Turn the paper round anticlockwise so that the unseen staple is nearest you; insert the stapler *between* the paper and staple the top paper only—in other words, there are now two staples on this part of the paper, one on top and one below. Turn the paper once more and genuinely staple the remaining side. You can now turn the paper packet over and show both sides—the coin is seen to be securely stapled in. After having asked someone to feel that it is there, hold it as shown in Fig. 58E and secretly allow the coin to slide out into the hand. Turn the hand over at this instant and lay the now empty paper on the table. The audience will think it is still there because the outline impression shows plainly. You can now dispose of the coin so that it will appear elsewhere (see next trick). When ready to vanish the coin, simply pick up the paper and tear into little bits.

COIN IN THE NEST OF PURSES

AFTER a marked coin disappears (see 'Stapled Coin' and 'Fade-away Coin' on pages 64 and 62), the spectator is handed a zip purse. When he opens it, there is another purse inside also zipped up. This is opened and he finds yet another purse inside this one. Inside this the spectator discovers a matchbox bound with elastic bands. Inside this box is a small sealed bag, and inside this is the actual borrowed and marked coin!

In addition to the three zip purses (which are quite ordinary, except that they must nest inside each other), you will require a matchbox and a little bag made of cloth, about 1 inch by 2 and open at one end. There is also a special slide made of tin—rather like a flat tube. This is about 3 inches long and just large enough to allow a coin easily to slide down it (see Fig. 59).

To set the trick up, place the bag over the end of the

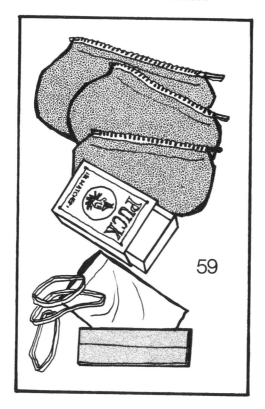

59

slide and secure with an elastic band. Insert this into the box, and again secure with bands. The box is placed in the smallest purse with the tube protruding and zipped up as far as possible. This is in turn put in the larger purse and zipped up and, finally, put into the largest purse. The set-up is now placed in the pocket, tube uppermost (Fig. 60).

The method of working is simple. All you do after having secretly secured the coin is to drop it into the slide which you then pull out of the purse. Zip up the purse and

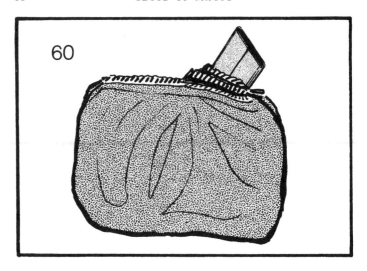

lay it on the table. The audience think the coin is still in the
stapled paper, so you pretend to vanish it. Pick up the purse,
showing your hands otherwise empty, and unzip and withdraw the next purse. Cover the unzipped section with the
fingers and appear to unzip the whole length of it. Withdraw
the last purse—do the same. Allow the spectator to reach in
and take out the box. He unwraps it and finds the bag, and
discovers the coin inside.

Naturally, everything can be passed for minute
inspection. A more sophisticated version of the slide has a
funnel-shaped top. This simply enables you to locate the top
or opening of the slide more positively. This is shown in
Fig. 61. Notice the pin which allows the slide to be fastened
to the lining of the pocket. All you do here is simply to pull
the purses away from the tube bringing them into view in
one continuous movement—the tube remains behind without you really touching it.

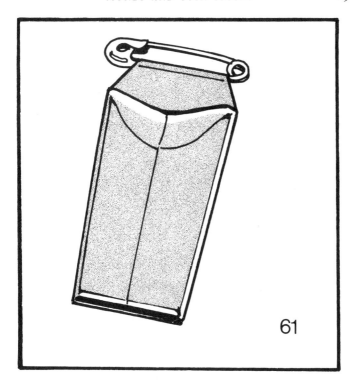

61

SHORT CHANGE

THIS was shown to our English party on a visit to a magic Convention in Amsterdam by an unknown German conjuror using French francs. It has since been discovered that this is a little-known move used by unscrupulous grafters, pitchmen, market traders, etc. in order to short-change their unsuspecting customers! I performed it on television a short while ago and was surprised by the interest it aroused.

Effect   Seven coins, all of one denomination, are shown,

and a spectator is asked to hold out his hand palm upwards. You tell him that you are going to count the coins onto his hand one by one and that as soon as the last one is put there he is to close his hand quickly so that you are unable to take one away again. This is done—the coins are slowly counted onto his hand, yet no matter how quickly he reacts, you are still able to leave him with only six coins. The effect can be repeated several times.

Required   A number of coins of like kind; these can be borrowed if desired to assure that they are not faked in any way. Seven is a convenient number to use, but experiment to find the number most suited to you.

Method   The secret is remarkably simple, and just as easy to do. You begin by openly showing the coins, allowing the spectators to see that there are in fact only seven and that your hands are otherwise empty. These are placed on your face-up left palm. The spectator holds his hand out palm upwards, and with your right forefinger and thumb you pick up the first coin and place it on his palm counting 'one', pick up the next one and put it with the first, counting 'two', and so on with the third, fourth and fifth coins (see Fig. 62).

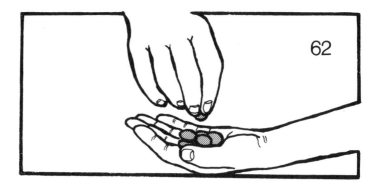

Pick up the sixth coin and place it in his hand as with the others, *but do not let it fall—immediately bring it away again.* Be sure to let it touch the others so that the same sound is heard. You count 'six'. At the same time you raise your left hand which still contains the last coin and openly drop it into his hand saying 'seven'. You retain this sixth coin in your right hand (see Fig. 63).

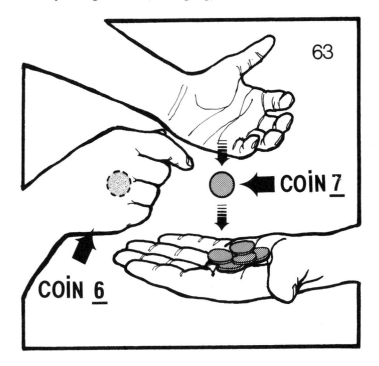

If he fails to close his hand quickly, do it for him at this point. He will be convinced anyway that he has all the coins safely in his hand . . . until he counts to find that he has only six.

Now you can reveal that you have the odd one. Repeat

the trick two or three times, but always be sure to misdirect by drawing attention to the last coin being dropped from your left hand into his—remember that this is the only coin not *put* into his hand: it is actually dropped in. The psychology is that he is always keen to close his hand in order not to miss the last one, but misses the fact that the sixth coin is not really deposited in his hand—you only pretend to do so.

TRANSPO COINS

A SILVER coin is wrapped in a handkerchief and it changes places with a copper coin, which is similarly wrapped; both are held by a spectator. Then they are both wrapped together and the two coins change to seven separate coins.

This trick is in two parts—the first is the transposition of the silver and copper coins. Begin by having a copper coin palmed loosely in the right hand; then borrow a copper coin and a silver one. Take a hanky and spread it over the left hand. Pick up the silver coin between the thumb and forefinger of the right hand. Appear to drop the silver coin into the hanky, but allow the copper one to fall instead, letting the silver coin drop loosely against the curled fingers of the right hand.

At the same time grasp the coin through the hanky with the left hand and turn this hand over, but still hold the coin, now covered, between the finger and thumb of the left hand. Wrap the material round tightly below the coin and pass it to someone to hold firmly, saying 'Here's the silver coin.' Still with the silver coin palmed in the right hand, pick up the visible copper coin and repeat the same moves with another hanky, this time switching the silver coin for the copper coin. Someone is invited to hold this as you say

'And here is the copper coin.' Make a magic pass and, when the hankies are unwrapped, the coins will be seen to have changed place. Take the opportunity of disposing of the spare coin at this stage.

For the second part, you will need to have seven copper coins already in your left pocket. While attention is focused on unwrapping the hankies, secure these coins and hold them in a stack concealed in your left hand. Pick up one of the hankies and hold it, spread by two corners, with the finger and thumb of each hand. Pass the left hand under the hanky while the right spreads the hanky over the now outstretched left palm (covering the unknown coins).

Openly lay the copper coin and the silver coin on the centre of the hanky. The left finger and thumb grasp these coins from under the hanky. Say that you will now cause the two coins to penetrate the cloth. Bring over the forward corner of the hanky with the right hand; as it passes over the two coins they are nipped between the finger and thumb and, as the right hand nears the top breast pocket, they are secretly dropped in—at the same time, and in one continuous movement, uncover the left hand to reveal the seven coins and drop them one by one onto the table, counting them as you do so.

UNDERCOVER DETECTIVE

WHILE the performer's back is turned, a spectator places a coin under one of three little caps or covers already on the table. On turning round, the magician is immediately able to divine which cover hides the coin. This can be repeated several times.

The standard and perhaps more widely known method is with the use of a prepared coin. This coin has been faked by sticking a small piece of hair to one edge—this,

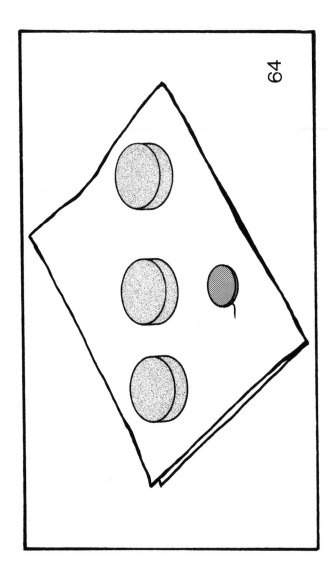

unseen by the audience, will provide the clue to where the coin is. Where you see the hair peeking out—that's where the coin is. To make the hair prominent it has been thickened, but of course it would normally be virtually invisible (Fig. 64).

The spectators will want to examine the covers and the coin, so while they are looking at the covers, drop the coin in your pocket. Ask for the loan of another coin and, since it has obviously been borrowed, it will be free from deception. You can now repeat the trick ad lib—but you now use a different principle altogether.

The covers are really plastic caps taken from plastic containers normally used to contain screws and other small items. Select them with care and you will have a really baffling mystery always available. Keep the containers, because you will be able to perform a very fine trick with them (see 'Plop', page 106). The covers should be placed on a light surface such as a white sheet of paper or tablecloth. If a coin is placed under one of them, this cover will appear *just an infinitesimal shade darker*. It will take a little practice to tell which one, but it is almost impossible for anyone not in the know to detect the secret—and that's how it's done. In no time at all you will be able to spot the correct cover with 100 per cent accuracy.

CHAPTER SEVEN

Miscellaneous Effects

BALANCING MATCH

Effect An ordinary match is balanced on end on your thumb-nail (Fig. 65). This is not an extravagant trick of course, only a stunt, but it can be quite a puzzler. The spectators will naturally try it, but they always fail even if they moisten the end of their match. They can actually remove your match from your thumb while it is still balancing—they will be certain you are using some sort of adhesive!

Secret This is very little known; all you do is unobtrusively to rub the bottom of the match against the face of one of your back teeth. The small amount of protective film which coats the teeth will enable you to balance the match, even on an unsteady hand.

COLOUR CHANGE MATCHES

Two matches are held upright between the tips of the left finger and thumb. The right fingertips now approach and apparently pull the heads right off the matches. The audience, however, suspect that all you did was turn them over. So, very slowly and openly, reverse them and to everyone's surprise the heads are now seen to be entirely different colours.

Unknown to the spectators, you have two extra matches with different coloured heads, say red and blue. They

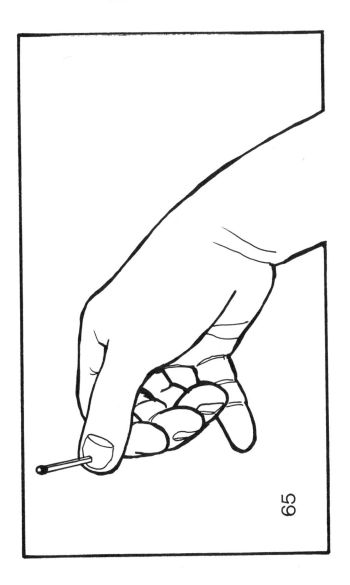

65

are held heads down by the right thumb against the side of the first finger of the right hand, as shown in Fig. 66. As stated, the other two matches with brown heads are held heads upwards between the thumb and forefinger of the left hand. The pictures show the view as seen by the performer, and of course the audience must not suspect the presence of the coloured matches in the right hand.

The right hand approaches the left, and while the fingers cover the matches, you make a pretence of pulling the heads off the brown ones, but making it obvious that you are turning them over. What you really do, however, is to switch the brown-headed ones for the coloured ones. This is done quite simply as you bring the hands together; under cover of the right fingers, allow the left thumb and finger to grip the coloured-headed matches, releasing them with the right. At the same time, grip the brown-headed ones with the right finger and thumb, carrying them away, turning half right as you do so; drop them in your pocket or, if seated, let them fall on your lap. Fig. 67 shows the precise moment when the two sets of matches are exchanged, while Fig. 68 shows the right hand withdrawing the switched pair. Still draw attention to the now supposedly reversed matches and, after being challenged, turn them round to show they have heads of a different colour altogether; your hands are shown otherwise perfectly empty.

RATTLING GOOD TRICK

THIS is a 'rattling' good trick to try on your friends! You show them three matchboxes, but only one of these contains matches—this is rattled to prove it. The matchboxes are placed in a row on the table and then you begin to move them

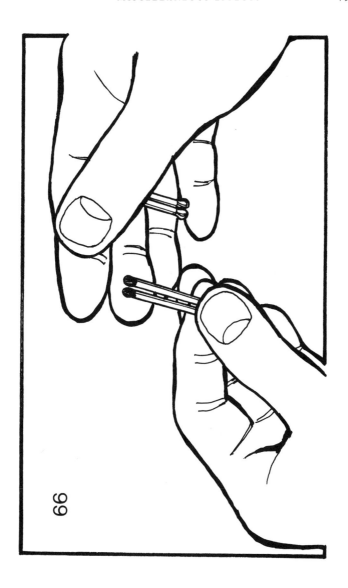

66

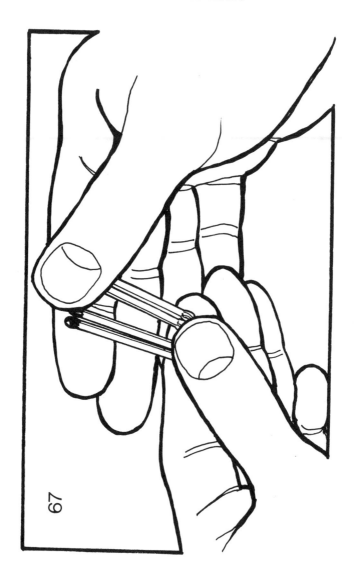

67

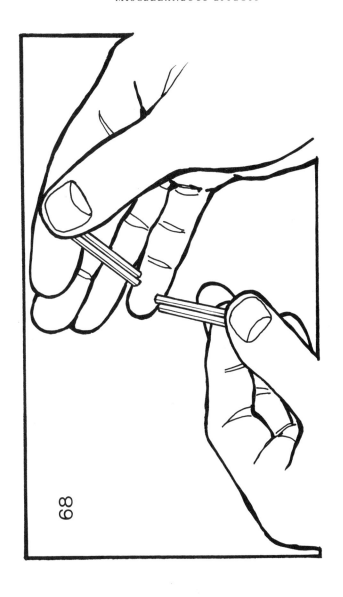

around, altering and changing their positions. Ask the spectator to see if he can follow the position of the box which contains the matches. Even though he watches very carefully, he is always wrong.

How is it done? 'It might be magic.' Well, it isn't really because you secretly have another matchbox and this contains a few matches. The existence of this extra box is unsuspected by the audience because it is fastened to your right wrist by an elastic band and it is up your sleeve out of sight. When you are ready to work the trick, pick up one of the boxes with the right hand and shake it. They hear the noise of the matches being rattled and think it comes from the box they can see. The other two boxes are shaken with the left hand. Slowly move them around changing their positions. When your friend picks out the 'rattling' box you pick it up with the left hand and shake it to prove he is wrong and instantly pick up another with the right hand and shake it to prove where the rattle box 'really is'.

To finish the trick quite effectively, place one of the empty boxes in your pocket. Then rattle one of the remaining two. Say that you will now cause the matches to pass from the box on the table into the box in your pocket. Pick up the box and show it empty and then, reaching into your pocket, take out the other box and show it to be full of matches. This last part can be omitted if you like but it does make quite a good finish. All you need is a duplicate box of matches already in your pocket and it is this box you take out at the end.

NB   To make the 'rattle' more pronounced, place a small piece of tin foil in the concealed matchbox.

TOPSY-TURVY MATCHBOX

YOU will need to make a specially faked matchbox—this is

easily done by cutting the tray part into two halves. Assemble them in the drawer section so that one half is reversed. The matchbox should be the type that has an identical label on each side. You will also need another box which is similar in appearance but which is in fact perfectly ordinary. They both have matches inside.

Begin by showing the two boxes. Have a friend pick up one of the boxes. If he picks up the faked box ask him to hand it to you, but if he picks up the ordinary box let him keep it while you pick up the other one. You will see that, whatever happens, you have the faked box. Now tell him he is to do as you do. Hold your box as if you were going to open it. He does the same. Turn it over lengthways, then sideways and all ways, so that although he follows you closely he never seems to finish exactly as you do—because when you each push your drawers open, they will be different. His box will be upside down and yours the right way up, or vice versa. The closer he follows you the more bewildered he will be when you each finally open your box. As a comic finish, contrive to make him end up with his box upside down. You open yours, look him straight in the face, tell him to open his, and all the matches fall out!

WHO'LL BUY THE DRINKS?

PRINT or type four cards similar to those illustrated in Fig. 69. If you carry them around in your pocket, you can always be certain of having a little fun at your friend's 'expense'. The four cards are shown face down, the idea being to get your friend to select the No. 3 card ('I will'). Follow the method and you ought not to fail.

Arrange the cards face down from the top:

(1) 'Care for a drink?'
(2) 'That's a good idea'

69

(3) 'I will'

(4) 'Who'll buy the drinks?'

(*a*) State that you are going to show him a card trick. You deal out the four cards face down from left to right, commencing with the top card No. 1. Ask him to place a finger on any card and, if he touches No. 3, you turn over cards 1, 2 and 4 in that order. He turns his card up and finds the drinks are on him. Incidentally, the odds are that most people will, in fact, point to No. 3 (three in a row of four).

(*b*) If, however, he does *not* touch the 'I will' card the first time, get him to touch another, and if the 'I will' card is the second one touched, draw the other two untouched cards towards yourself and get him to make a second choice of one of his two cards he originally touched. If he touches the 'I will' card, push it towards him. If he touches the other, pull it towards you saying, 'This leaves the last card to you.'

(*c*) But supposing he first touches two different cards, other than the 'I will' card; well, pull these back towards yourself, then get him to select one of the two remaining and proceed as in (*b*) above. Whatever the result, he will always end up with the 'I will' card.

The above is, of course, simply a comedy version of using the 'Conjuror's Choice' principle, which can be adapted in many other effects where you require to 'force' a certain object out of several.

VANISHING PEN

Now here is a real dandy of a trick, because it happens 'right before their very eyes'. Hand someone a piece of paper together with a ball-point pen and tell him to sign his name on the paper. Now roll the pen inside the paper, twisting both ends so that the pen is safely secured inside. Then 'hey

presto!'—the paper is immediately torn in two and the pen
has completely vanished. There is, of course, no question
that the pen and paper are other than ordinary because the
spectator has actually handled and used both. It is usually
better to allow spectators to 'examine' props in an indirect
way, rather than inviting them to 'examine them closely'.
It is possible that, in your next trick, the apparatus you want
to use will not bear such close scrutiny, yet the audience may
want to 'examine' these closely too.

But let's get down to the 'know-how' of the vanishing
pen effect. It is really quite ingenious. You will need a ball-
point pen, the type with a loose cap as shown in Fig. 70.

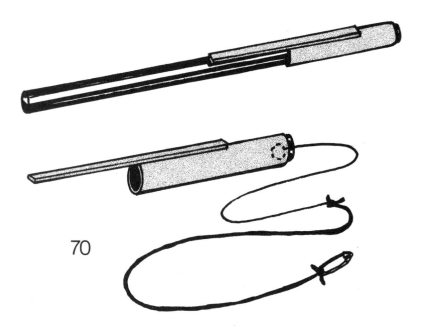

70

It is the cap only that has been faked. First of all, drill a small hole in the extreme tip. Tie a small bead to about 6 inches of nylon fishing line. Thread the nylon through the hole so the bead is inside the cap. Now tie the end of the nylon to a piece of black cord elastic (the length of this should be about 10 inches but it can be determined by trial and error). Fasten a safety-pin to the end of the elastic—all this is illustrated in the sketch. The pin is secured to the inside of the jacket just above the sleeve opening—the elastic is passed down the sleeve where the cap dangles in an easily accessible position.

To present the effect, hand the pen and paper to a spectator requesting him to sign his name on the sheet of paper. Incidentally, the size of the paper should be about 8 inches by 4. While this is being done, secretly secure the cap, holding it at the extreme tips of the left-hand fingers. Take back the pen and insert it into the cap. Pick up the paper and roll it round the pen forming a sort of loose tube; twist the paper at the far end. Ask the spectator to feel the pen inside the paper; as soon as he has done so, allow the elastic to pull the pen up the sleeve. Now turn the tube round and twist the paper at the other end. The trick is now done—tear the tube in half and the pen has completely vanished.

PATRIOTIC POTS

THIS is an extremely simple effect, ideal to perform before audiences of all ages, and because the plot is straightforward, it is easily understood by the very young. It is, in its way, a classic trick, highly visual and sustaining the spectators' attention from start to finish. One is tempted to carry on eulogizing about this trick, rather like the descriptions in the magic dealer's catalogue which uses such epithets as 'no skill needed', 'easy to do', 'everything examined', 'can be performed close up', 'no preparation', 'has a surprise finish', etc. It so happens that all this is true and, incidentally, the cost of the props is negligible. Props consist of three plastic flower-pots—one painted red, one white and the other blue; also three each of red, white and blue 9-inch-square paper tissues.

The pots are placed in a row on the table as in Fig. 71 (your view), blue to the left, white in the centre and red on

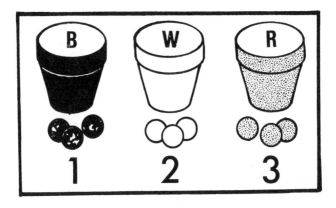

71

the right. The audience see them from left to right as red, white and blue. Take up the tissue-paper squares and roll each into a ball, placing one of each colour in each of the three pots. So that the audience can be certain of this, tip them out into three groups onto the table so that you have a red, white and blue ball in front of each pot. To make the moves easy to follow, I will refer to the red pot as R pot (shaded), the white pot as W pot and the blue as B pot (solid black). The three groups from right to left will be groups 1, 2 and 3, while the balls will be designated as the red ball, white ball or blue ball. Fig. 72 should make this clear—in this case it is as seen from the audience's point of view.

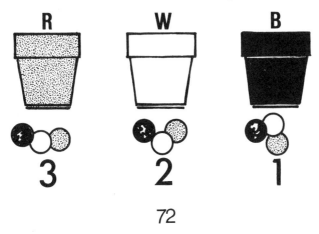

72

There are two easy sleights to master (the finger palm and the switch) and these are described at the end of the trick.

(1) Go to group 1 and pick up the red ball in the right hand while the left hand tilts the R pot forward towards the audience; the red ball is dropped in the R pot. This is what the audience think you do, but in reality, as soon as the hand is in the pot out of sight, you finger-palm the ball and, unknown to them, secretly take it out again.

(2) The right hand (with the red ball palmed) goes to group 1, picks up the white ball and drops it into the W pot. Actually you allow the red ball to drop instead, while the white ball is finger-palmed.

(3) The right hand (with the white ball palmed) picks up the blue ball from group 1 and appears to drop it into B pot.

Again you do the switch and drop the palmed white ball instead, retaining the blue. This uses up the three balls from group 1—so turn your attention to group 2.

(4) The right hand (with blue ball palmed) picks up the red ball from group 1. This is apparently dropped into the pot (but, as before, the palmed ball, this time blue, is dropped instead).

(5) Right hand (with the red ball palmed) picks up the white ball from group 2 and *actually drops it into the pot* (this time there is no switch).

(6) With the red ball palmed, the right hand picks up the blue ball from the second group and appears to drop it into the B pot (again the switch takes place, leaving you with the blue ball palmed).

(7) Blue ball still palmed, the red ball is picked from the third group and it is *actually dropped into R pot* (blue ball is still palmed).

(8) Pick up white ball from group 3 and appear to drop it into W pot (but do the switch leaving the blue one instead).

(9) Lastly, pick up the remaining blue ball *and actually drop it into the B pot* (while the white ball is still palmed in the right hand).

To recapitulate: You have (as far as the audience is concerned) simply taken all three balls of one colour and dropped them into the same colour pot. In order to bring the trick to its climax, pick up the R pot with the right hand allowing the palmed white ball secretly to drop in and, almost in the same movement, turn the pot over to reveal three balls of different colours—instead of all the same colour as the audience expect. Now turn over the white pot and tip out the three balls, and lastly the B pot. The audience now see that the colours have paradoxically come together again.

Although this effect takes longer to describe than to perform and requires practice to do it smoothly, the effort involved makes its learning well worth while. Of course you could use balls made of wool or sponge, and, instead of pots, paper bags or pudding basins.

The finger-palm is very simply done and is useful in many other tricks. The fingers are slightly curled towards the palm and held naturally, while the third and little fingers loosely support the concealed ball. Learn to do it without looking at the hand.

The other ball is picked up between the forefinger and thumb; as soon as it is out of sight in the pot, allow the palmed ball to drop, at the same time rolling the other ball into the finger-palmed position. Practice is essential until you can do it without hesitation and without looking. This is known as a *switch* and again is useful in many other effects.

THE FABULOUS 'PADDLE' MOVE

OF all the close-up tricks ever invented, it is almost a certainty that tricks involving the 'paddle' move are the most widely used. Fig. 73 will give you some idea of just a few of the large variety of versions available. You will notice that besides the 'paddles' of various kinds there are dice, pen-knives, cocktail sticks, pencils and so on; all of these, as you will see later, can be manipulated using the paddle move.

What is the 'paddle' move? Well, it is the ability to show the same side of the 'paddle' twice when the spectators think they are seeing both sides. This is accomplished by rolling the handle of the paddle between the fingers at the precise moment that the hand is turned over to show the opposite side. Done neatly, it is absolutely undetectable.

In this particular version we make use of two flat sticks; they can be made of wood or plastic—those in the

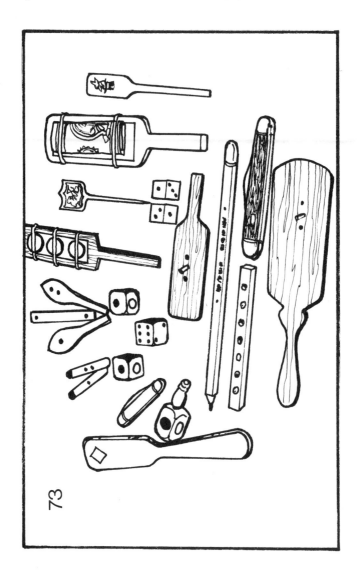

73

drawing are made to represent large matches and they are about 2 inches long by $\frac{1}{4}$ inch wide and about $\frac{1}{8}$ inch in thickness. These measurements, however, are not critical so long as the paddle move can be executed with them. Paint or stick a spot on one side of one stick leaving the opposite side blank. The other stick has one spot on one side and two spots on the other (see Fig. 74). The basic effect is that the two sticks are shown blank; then first one spot appears, then another, and they multiply and vanish and hop from one stick to another in a most inexplicable fashion.

First of all, though, let us deal with the paddle move. Follow the directions with a stick in your hand and you will soon find that just a little practice will make you perfect. Hold one of the sticks at one end between the finger and thumb of the right hand, palm uppermost, and you are now ready to begin. The move is really in two parts, the 'twist' and the 'roll'.

The twist By merely turning over the hand towards the body, using a wrist movement so that the palm is now downwards, the stick or paddle will now point to the body, thus showing the opposite side. This is a perfectly natural move but must be done at the same time as the 'roll' is executed, and this is as follows.

The roll It works by simply pushing the right thumb to the left, allowing the stick to turn over, and, reversing the move, allowing the stick to roll back to the right.

Practise both the twist and the roll separately, then execute both moves at the same time, and you will discover the illusion to be perfect. Although it seems to the onlooker that both sides have been shown, you have in reality shown

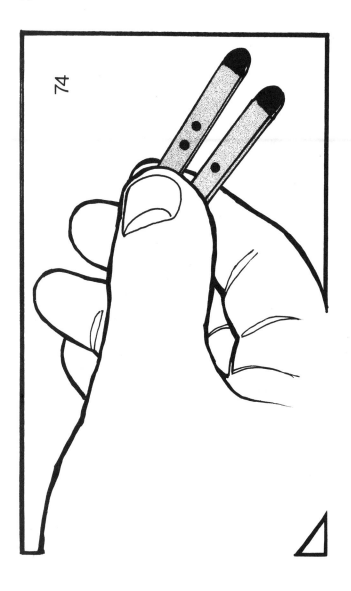

the same side twice. Endeavour to execute the paddle move with both hands; also, if possible, try to hold two sticks between the finger and thumb and twist both together.

Preparation Secure the two sticks with an elastic band, single spots inwards. When ready, remove them from your pocket with the blank side facing upwards; then remove the band.

Routine Hold both sticks at the middle between the thumb and finger of the left hand, blank side uppermost as in Fig. 75. Note that the top stick conceals the single spot on the lower one. The right finger and thumb withdraw the top stick, while the left thumb rests over the spot on the lower stick, concealing it (Fig. 76). By means of the basic paddle move, show both sides apparently blank. Fig. 77 also shows the first part of the paddle move. Rub the single-spot stick under the left sleeve, turning it over to reveal the spot. Show the other side still blank by means of the 'twist' only. Rub this under the left sleeve, turning it over to reveal the spot on the 'other' side (Fig. 78). Now show a spot on *both* sides by means of the basic move.

Rub the 'spot' (blank side) onto the other stick, removing the left thumb to reveal the spot. Two sticks are now showing a spot on each. Show that the single-spot stick is blank on one side, then 'rub off' the spot on the sleeve and show that it has 'arrived' on the other stick (basic move to show one spot on each side).

Next, cause a spot to appear on the single-spot stick; show *both* sticks on 'both sides' so that each stick has one spot on each side. Hold a stick in each hand to execute this.

Now cause the spot to hop from one stick to the other; by using the 'roll', make the left stick appear with two spots

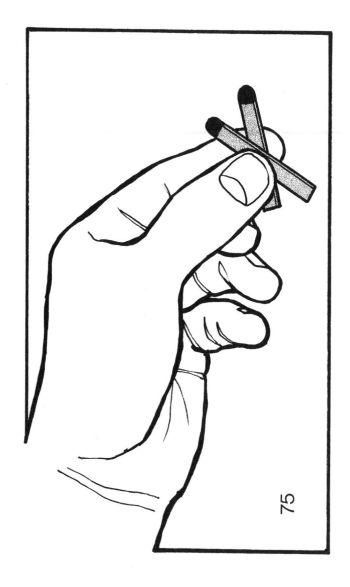

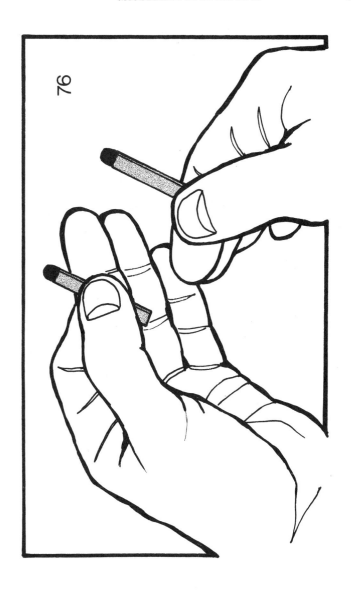

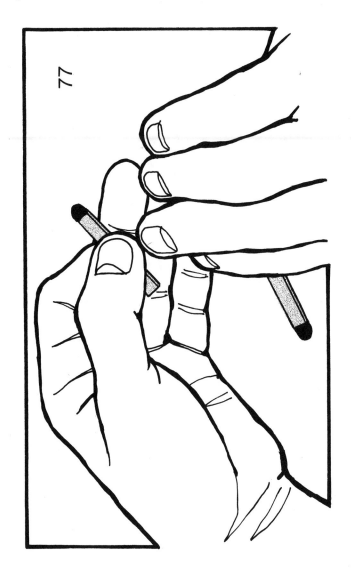

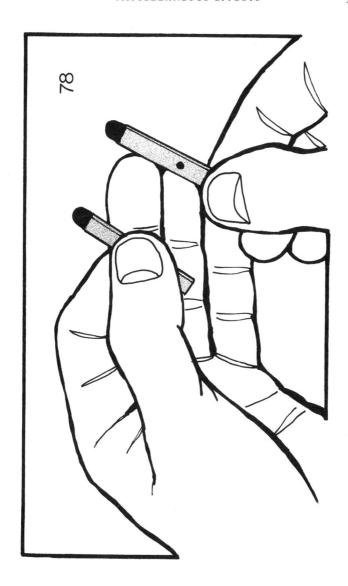

and the right stick become blank. Lay aside the two-spot stick and cause a spot to appear on one side of the blank stick. *Pass this one out for inspection.*

Pick up the two-spot stick, show that it has two spots on each side, 'wipe' one off from one side and then pass it for inspection. Finally continue with a series of 'hopping' spots and 'wiping-off' moves and finish by restoring them to one spot on each side of each stick.

DICEY

THE picture depicting the several paddle tricks (Fig. 73) shows one or two dice. They too can be used when doing the paddle move and it is accomplished in much the same way.

Hold the dice between the forefinger and thumb of the right hand, palm downwards. Turn the palm upwards in order to show the bottom face of the dice, but as you do so, 'roll' the dice one turn to the right so that the face which was against the ball of the forefinger will now show as the 'bottom' of the dice. Practise this, and when proficient practise using two dice.

You can, for example, let the spectators note the number of spots on top of the dice and then show them the bottom spots, but due to your secret move they see a different set of spots. Do it several times so that they see first the top number, then the 'bottom' numbers. Lay the dice on the table and turn them up slowly and the spots on the bottom will have changed.

STILL DICEY

USING two dice, let someone shake them in his hands and stack them one on top of the other. Look away while this is being done. You now tell him the total of the spots on the three hidden sides.

All you have to do is deduct the number of spots on the top side from fourteen and you have your answer. Or you can repeat the above with the two dice flat on the table— simply deduct the total of the two top sides from fourteen as before.

This is brought about by the fact that all dice should have their opposite sides totalling seven, i.e. a five opposite a two, a six opposite a one and so on.

On visiting Pompeii recently, the ancient Roman city buried 2000 years ago beneath the lava of the erupting volcano Mount Vesuvius, I noticed several dice which had been discovered during the excavations. They were probably made of ivory, but otherwise they were almost identical to their present-day counterparts. The Pompeiians certainly played dice games with them, but one wonders if they also knew about doing conjuring tricks with them . . . I am sure they did.

LINKING MINT

BEFORE appearing in front of your audience, break a 'mint with a hole' into two and stick it together again by moistening it, at the same time linking another one into it. Have these ready in your pocket. Offer someone a mint from the packet, meanwhile securing the linked ones in your hand. Taking out another two mints from the packet, place them in the hand containing the linked ones, give them a gentle squeeze and drop the linked pair on the table. As you put the packet back in your pocket, dispose of the two loose ones.

Your audience will be quite surprised to see the two mints firmly linked together. This is just a 'quickie', but none-the-less quite effective.

THE KEY OF ENDOR

THE magician places a latch key on his hand and tells the

story of the Witch of Endor, who kept a princess imprisoned in the castle: the door could be opened only by a single hair taken from her golden locks. Her lover, the prince, possessed such a hair and used it in a most magical way in order to turn the key. The performer takes an imaginary hair and, in pantomime, slowly winds it round and round the key; by pulling on the end of the 'hair' the key slowly turns over.

It is all a question of balance—the key is held resting on the palm of the hand as shown in Fig. 79. If the hand is tilted forwards, the key will roll over, but the hand must be tilted imperceptibly and very slowly so that the key will roll over and over very slowly.

This looks most uncanny and, if the final turn of the key coincides with the imaginary pull on the hair, it looks quite creepy.

THE MECHANIC'S GHOST

MAGIC as a hobby has devotees from all walks of life and every trade, profession and science. It follows that ideas in magic are nurtured from this combined store-house of knowledge. Each year conjurors gather together at Conventions bent on showing each other their latest 'pet' effect. It is therefore hardly surprising that there is a constant stream of new effects going the rounds.

Some years ago the effect about to be described came out of the ideas bank. It was played around with by most conjurors but you seldom see it now. The effect is simple, direct and visual. The performer shows a nut and bolt lying on the palm of his hand; the nut is securely screwed onto the bolt. They are put into the spectator's hand and, when he looks at them, he finds the nut has become unaccountably unscrewed from the bolt.

Several versions appeared but, because of the special

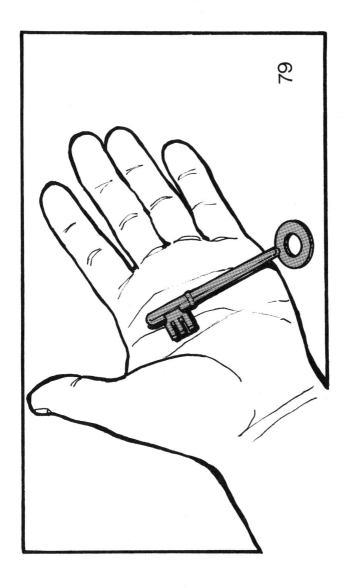

79

set-up, they lost popularity. In my version described, the effect is ready to perform without a lot of 'getting ready' and is a lot easier to do than most. The effect is basically the same, except that the performer begins by showing a plastic box—this is seen to contain a large nut and bolt, the nut being firmly screwed on to the bolt: attention is drawn to this fact. The box is now handed to someone to hold and after a suitable story to the effect that the 'mechanic's ghost lived in the box', etc., the spectator opens it to discover that the 'mechanic's ghost' has been to work and unscrewed the nut.

Fig. 80 depicts the apparatus, but to make it clear a transparent box has been used. A small hole the size of a pin-head is drilled in the bottom of the box. The nut and bolt must be easily unscrewed (keep them oiled). The head of the bolt should be round; a wing nut is shown, but a square nut will work just the same. You will also need a length of nylon fishing line (the thinnest possible); experiment, and you will find the length required. Tie a loop at one end large enough to insert a finger. Pass the other end up through the hole in the bottom of the box and wind it round the top of the bolt in a clockwise direction; again, the number of turns must be experimented with. Screw on the nut to about halfway, place the nut and bolt in the box and you are all set to go.

When ready, introduce the box by holding it in the left hand. The left forefinger engages in the nylon loop now protruding from the base of the box. Remove the lid and draw attention to the fact that the nut and bolt are well and truly screwed together (the nylon will be invisible). Replace the lid and, with the right hand, give the box to someone to hold. In the same instant, the left hand drops away pulling the nylon out of the box. This causes the bolt to turn round;

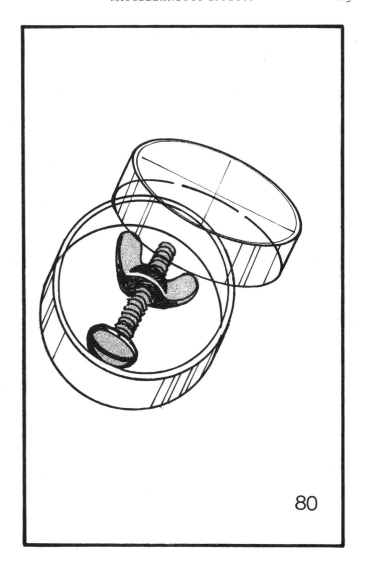

80

since the bolt head is round and the nut is square or wing-shaped, they will not turn and will automatically become unscrewed—they are in this condition when handed to the spectator. The nylon thread can be quietly dropped to the floor or otherwise disposed of.

Although I have omitted it for clarity, my box is padded with a piece of foam rubber (the nylon passes right through this), and any rattling is thus muffled. Make one up and have some fun playing around; who knows, you may come up with a new idea—you will never be short of an audience.

PLOP

EARLIER on in this book, I described a trick called 'Undercover Detective' (page 73). This made use of the round lids from small tubular clear plastic containers in which items such as pins and screws are sold.

The effect about to be described makes use of the container itself and the complete trick is very easily made. Show this plastic container (we will now rather grandly call it a 'vase') and place a steel washer on top of it rather like a lid. On top of the washer place two small coins, these being too large to pass through the hole in the washer. There is also a cardboard cylinder which fits loosely over the vase. Raise the cover so that the interior of the vase can be seen; give a little twist and the coins suddenly penetrate *through the washer* and tumble into the vase. Everything is given for inspection.

As already stated, the apparatus is easily made; it is a good idea, however, to glue a disc of, say, plastic or metal onto the bottom of the vase to glamorize the prop; it also makes it easy to handle. The cylinder is made from stiff card rolled into a tube—the diameter should be just a

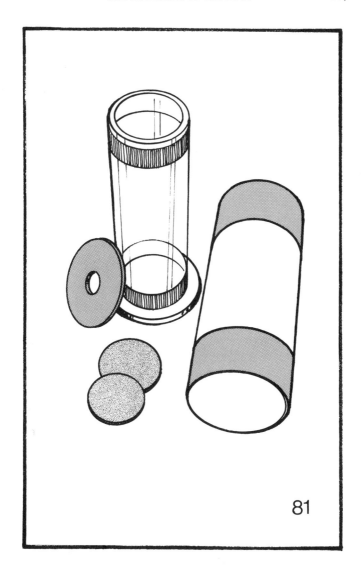

81

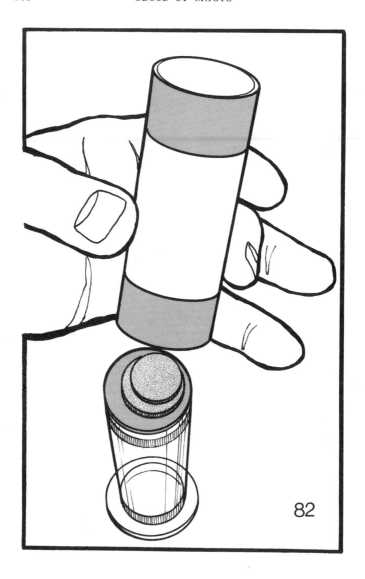

82

fraction larger than the washer. This tube is also decorated according to taste (see the outfit made up in Fig. 81).

Method and presentation First of all pass out everything for examination. Place the disc on top of the vase and then lay the borrowed coins on the disc as shown in Fig. 82. Raise the cover about half way so that the lower part of the vase is visible. In doing so, clip the disc inside the tube by pinching the sides very slightly and carry it up together with the coins. Give the vase a little twist; at the same time, release the pressure on the disc—it will turn over, shooting the coins into the vase, and then come to rest in its former position on top of the vase. The spectators see and hear the coins drop into the vase. Lower the cover and let them see that the disc is still in place. Be careful not to let them see into the top of the cover when the coins and disc are raised. The whole point is, of course, not to let the audience realize that the disc is being raised, and a suggested way to achieve this move is to lay the hand over the top of the cover and raise it by gripping it with the two outside fingers. A little practice will enable you to lift the cover and apply sufficient pressure to pinch in its sides in order to bring up the disc. A slight relaxing of the fingers will cause the disc to fall, turning over as it does so.

A very spectacular result can be achieved by using a steel ball-bearing instead of the coins.

NO SMOKING

PERHAPS this is the best way to stop smoking, because a packet filled with cigarettes will suddenly be seen to be empty!

The cigarette carton is prepared as follows. First, remove all the cigarettes and cut the tray right across about an inch from the bottom (see Fig. 83). Replace both sections of the cut tray in the outer packet and return the cigarettes. The smaller section should be at the bottom.

To show the box filled with cigarettes, *push* the tray up from the bottom. However, if you *pull* the tray up from the top only, the upper part of the tray comes up leaving the cigarettes behind and the packet seems to be empty. Keep the packet well tilted towards you so that the spectators do not glimpse the top of the cigarettes.

RING RELEASE

A TUBE about 3 inches long is enclosed at each end. It has a cord hanging down in a loop on which is threaded a solid ring. Without cutting the string or damaging the tube you are able to remove the ring and immediately pass everything for inspection.

The tube can be made of plastic, metal or even cardboard. Four holes are drilled near the ends as shown in Fig. 85. One of them is just a little larger than the others (shown at X). The reason for this will be apparent later. Close the ends with caps or corks. A piece of cord on which is threaded a solid ring is now laced through the tube as shown. The knot on the cord is just large enough to be pushed tightly into the large hole (see Fig. 85).

When you are ready to perform, hold the tube in your left hand, the fingers casually covering the string which lies along the length of the tube. Now grasp the ring between the finger and thumb of the right hand, allowing the tube to hang down as in Fig. 84. The ring is seen to be securely on the string and the spectators' attention is drawn to this. Place the outfit behind your back and pull out the knot from the large hole. This will enable the ring to fall off the string, and the tube will look like Fig. 86. Still behind your back,

83

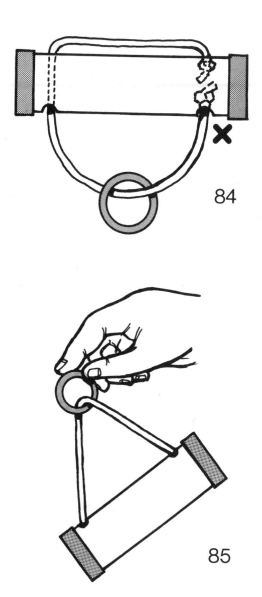

84

85

pull on the string which is lying along the tube. This loop
thus pulled will draw the loose end of string and the knot
into the tube so that it now appears as in Fig. 87. It is handed
in this condition to the spectators to examine.

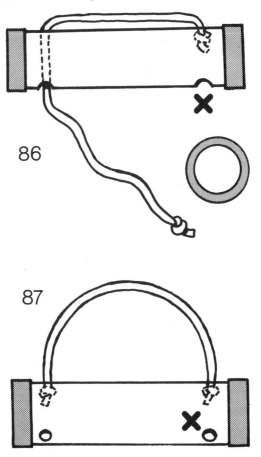

To reset the trick, remove one of the end-caps and draw out the knot, pushing it through the large hole opposite. Thread on the ring and finally poke the knot into the other hole at the opposite end of the tube. The set-up will now appear as in Fig. 84 once more.

THE MARK

A SIMPLE design such as a cross, circle or initial is pencilled on a sugar cube by a spectator. The cube is dropped into a cup of coffee or tea and the spectator holds his hand over the cup. The design mysteriously rises through the liquid to transfer itself, particle by particle, to the spectator's palm. Turning over his hand, he finds to his astonishment that this has happened.

Misdirection plays an important part in this little miracle—the method to bring about the effect is very simple. After having the sugar cube marked (it must be done with a lead pencil, incidentally), ask the spectator to place both hands, palms upwards, before him. Pick up the cube between the finger and thumb of your right hand, the mark showing uppermost (Fig. 88). Place it on the spectator's hand, but as you do so, roll the cube so that the face which bears the design comes against the ball of your thumb; slight pressure will secretly transfer the design to the thumb (see Fig. 89). The thumb, of course, is held with the cross-side downwards so that the spectator will not realize what has happened. Look him straight in the eye as you do this in order to distract his attention. Taking hold of the spectator's other hand, put it palm downwards and direct it to a position a few inches over the steaming liquid. In doing so your thumb presses against his palm and, unknown to him, the design is yet again transferred. He drops the cube into the beverage and lowers his hand still further. Spin your yarn as the sugar

88

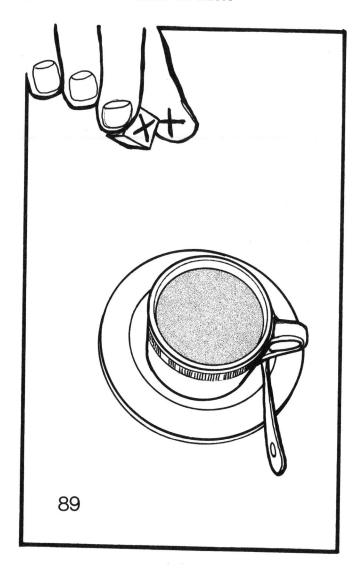

89

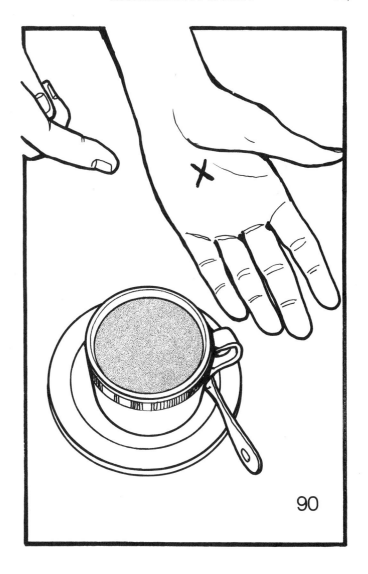

90

dissolves and, when he turns his hand palm uppermost, the design will be plainly seen (Fig. 90).

THREE LITTLE CUPS

THIS trick in its various forms is probably one of the oldest in the realm of magic. In fact, there is a picture of a person performing it inscribed on the walls of the burial chamber in Beni Hassan—and this dates back to 2500 BC.

Seneca (3 BC) wrote the following in the 42nd Epistle to Lucillus: 'It is in the very trickery that it pleases me, but show me how the trick is done and I have lost my interest therein.' Yet notwithstanding its antiquity, the 'Cups and Balls' trick, as it is generally known, is still popular today, and every country seems to have its own particular version. Indian conjurors, for instance, make use of a shape of cup as shown in Fig. 91 while others may use half coconut shells or even walnut shells. Modern conjurors, however, use cups made of metal as seen in Fig. 92. Notice the magic wand, the use of which also helps in the misdirection. Magicians the world over present the effect with varying degrees of

INDIAN CUPS & BALLS

91

92

skill; some use balls, lemons and various small objects which come and go under the 'cups' in an uncanny fashion. The 'gully gully' performers from the Near East even use live chicks.

In the very simple version about to be described, you will need no skill and require only three small plastic or metal cups, miniature flower-pots—even disposable drinking cups will suffice. These, together with four little cubes or balls cut from foam rubber, complete the apparatus. It will be easier to learn how to do this amazing little mystery if you follow the directions with the apparatus in your hands, trying out each stage of the effect as you come to it.

Effect Show the three cups together with three pieces of sponge. While stacking the cups upside down on the table, you cause the sponges to penetrate the cups one at a time; finally one of the sponges vanishes, to reappear under another cup placed a foot away. The secret lies in the presence of the fourth sponge, which is unknown to the audience. It is a good plan to equip yourself with a small stick or wand. This will assist in misdirection. It will also help you to follow the routine more easily if you name the cups A, B and C and stick a small label on each cup. It is necessary to do this only while actually learning the moves.

Begin by stacking the cups, mouths upward, as in Fig. 93 but with a sponge in the bottom of the centre cup (B); the remaining three sponges lie to one side on the table. Pick up the three cups and hold them, still mouths up, in your left hand. Remove the bottom cup (A) with the right hand, turn it over and set it mouth downwards to your right on the table. Repeat with cup B and place it in front of you, but remember that this has the secreted ball inside.

This is where the master move takes place; as the cup

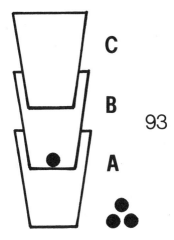

is taken with the right hand, turn it down smartly onto the table. The ball will remain in the cup, due to the pressure of air, and will be unsuspected by the spectators. Always set the cups down on the table in this way, whether they are empty or not, and remember to keep the mouths of the cups away from the audience. Be sure not to turn the cups down until they are close to the table.

There remains one cup (C) in the left hand—place this in the same way, mouth downwards, a little to the left of B. The position is now as in Fig. 94 except that the spectators think you have three *empty* cups on the table.

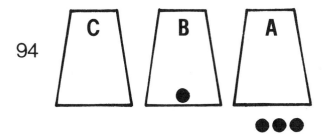

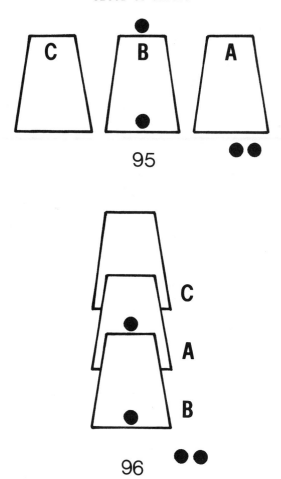

95

96

Place one of the three visible balls on top of the centre
cup (B) (see Fig. 95). Now place cup A on cup B, then cup C
on cup A, so that all three are stacked mouth downwards
(see Fig. 96). Tap the top cup with your wand and, with the

right hand, lift all three cups, turning them mouth upwards as you do so. This action reveals the ball which seems to have penetrated right through the cup. This ball is, of course, the one previously placed in cup B.

Leave this ball on the table and take the cups, mouths uppermost, in the left hand as before, repeating the same moves by placing the bottom cup (C) mouth downwards slightly to the right of the ball. Place the next cup, A (containing ball), over the visible ball (master move). Finally place cup B to the left of cup A. The situation is now as in Fig. 97. The spectators think there is only one ball under

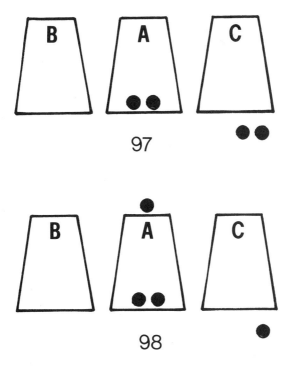

97

98

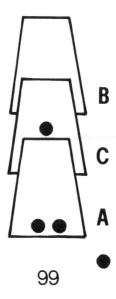

99

cup A (centre). Now put one of the two remaining visible balls on top of centre cup A (Fig. 98). Place cup C over cup A, then cup B over cup C, so that all are now stacked as before (Fig. 99). Tap with the wand and lift away the *three* cups to reveal two balls under the bottom cup.

Repeat the same moves by setting cup B to the right, cup C (containing the ball) over the two visible on the table and then cup A to the left (all mouth downwards, of course) (see Fig. 100). Place final ball on cup C, centre (Fig. 101). Now place cup B on cup C, followed by cup A on cup B (Fig. 102). Tap the top of the cups and lift the stack of three away, to reveal the three balls.

You are now back to exactly the same position as at the beginning with three cups all stacked—a ball secretly in cup B, while there are three visible balls on the table.

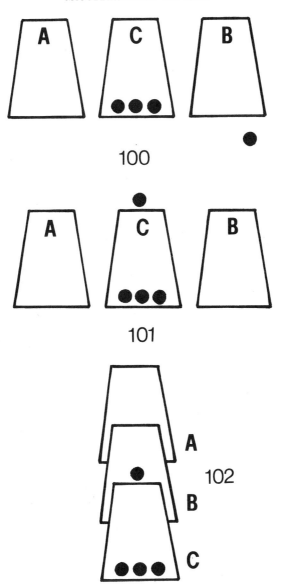

100

101

102

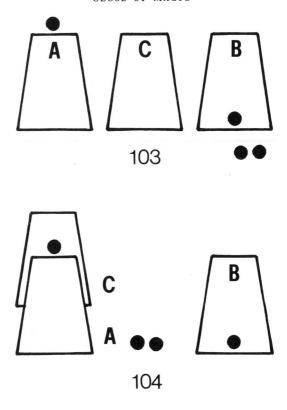

103

104

To conclude the routine, set the cups out as in Fig. 103, the ball being secretly under cup B to the right. A ball is visibly placed on cup A. Cover cup A with cup C (Fig. 104). Make a 'magic pass' over cups A and C and then lift these two cups together—but this time the ball has not 'penetrated'. However, on lifting cup B it is seen to have arrived there instead.

CHAPTER EIGHT

Silks, Bands and Ribbons

STRETCHING SILK

Q UITE an amazing effect can be obtained by following this procedure with a silk handkerchief. The illusion of apparently stretching the silk is also quite amusing.

Begin by holding the silk by its two top corners as in Fig. 105. Then lay it flat on the table or across your knee

105

and fold the two bottom corners up to the top corners (Fig. 106). Hold the silk directly in front of you, grasping the four corners, two in each hand (Fig. 107). The left hand now pulls on the corner (a) farthest away from the body while the right hand releases its opposite corner (b). At the same time the right hand pulls on the corner (c), the left hand releasing its opposite corner (d) (Fig. 108).

Secretly gather up a little of the ends of the silk in each hand, simultaneously twisting the silk and appearing to stretch it (Figs. 109 and 110). Continue the stretching action, releasing a little of the stock of silk from each hand as you do so, and you will find that you can apparently stretch the silk to quite an amazing length.

109

110

MYSTERY KNOTS

Two silk handkerchiefs are tied together by a spectator and the magician merely covers the knot with the folds of one of the hankies and immediately the silks are seen to be untied. The secret is simple, but most simple effects achieve the best results.

Be sure that the spectator ties a reef or square knot. By merely pulling both ends of the same hanky you pull out the knot and one hanky can be slid off the other. A good plan is to use two silks of different colours. Also, be careful to slip off the knot under cover of folding the knot into the folds of the hanky.

Get someone to hold this 'knot' and watch his face when you pull away one of the silks and show it to be completely untied. Figs. 111, 112 and 113 show the 'square' knot being tied. As you can see, it is quite a straightforward knot and most people tie in this fashion. But Fig. 114 shows what happens when two parts of the same silk are pulled.

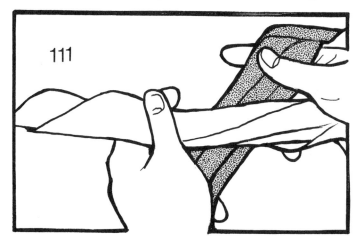

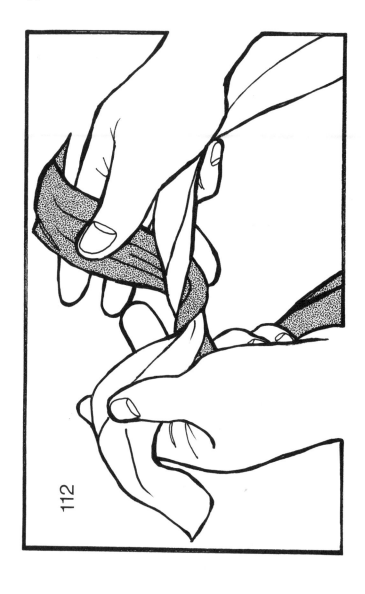

113

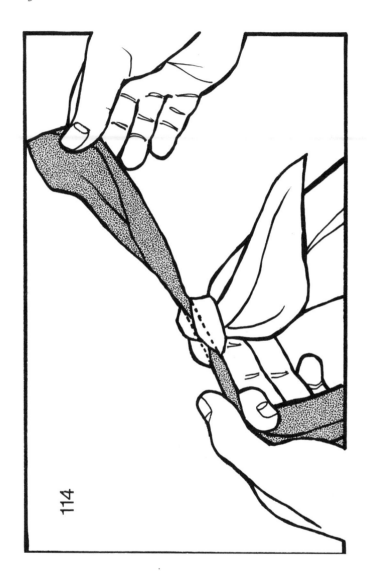

114

The left hand pulls the main part of the patterned silk away
to the left; the right fingers have pulled the right corner of
the same silk away to the right. This has the effect, as you can
see by close inspection of the picture, of causing the patterned
silk to straighten out. The other plain silk is now merely
wrapped around the patterned one, and in this position
it can easily be slipped off. This is done under the cover of
its own folds, the knot being pulled right off the end of
the patterned one.

FLIP-OVER BANDS

ELASTIC bands are universally obtainable so the apparatus for
this trick is easily available and at little or no cost. They
are easy to carry around in the pocket or to borrow, so the
trick can be worked at any time. To achieve such a puzzling
effect with such commonplace articles makes 'Flip-over
Bands' quite intriguing. There are several parts to this trick
as follows.

(1) An elastic band is looped over the first two fingers, the
hand is rapidly closed and opened again, and the band
mysteriously flips across to encircle the third and fourth
fingers.

(2) Again the hand is closed and the band flips back to its
former position.

(3) Now two different coloured bands are used and these are
placed one round the first and second fingers, the other
round the third and fourth. This time they change places.

(4) Finally, ostensibly to prove that the bands do not come
off the finger, another large band is intertwined round all
the fingers. Even with this restriction, the bands change
places, then pop back again to their original position.

Effect No. 1   Hold your left hand with its back to the

audience, palm towards yourself, and place an elastic band
round the first two fingers (Fig. 115). The right forefinger

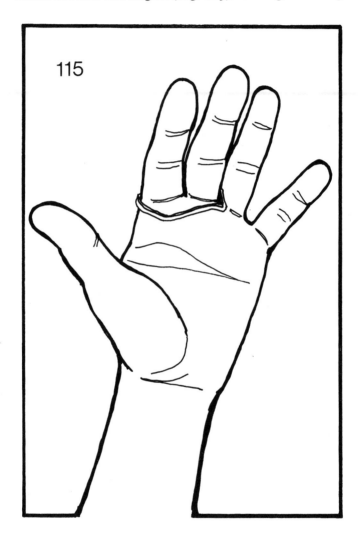

115

takes the band and stretches it towards you (Fig. 116). Now
bend down all the fingers into the palm, the right forefinger

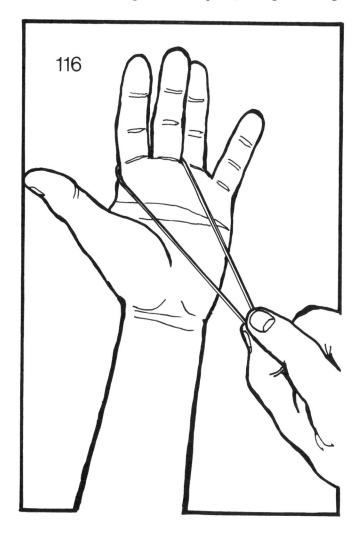

releasing the band so that it now encircles them (Fig. 117).
Open the hand and the band will now fly automatically to
encircle the third and smallest finger (Fig. 118).

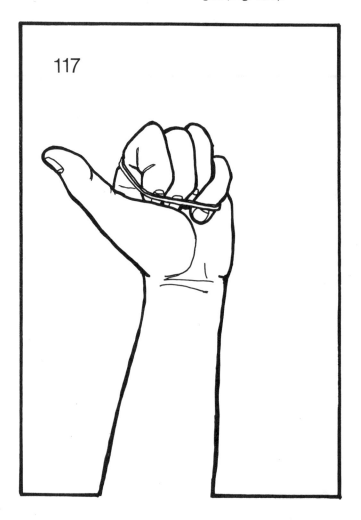

117

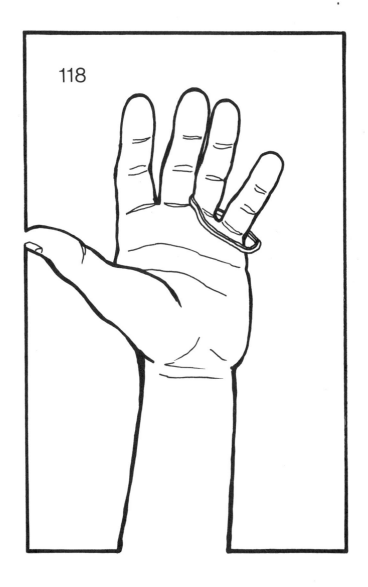

118

Effect No. 2   Reach over with the left thumb and insert it into the band which you open out towards you. Bend down your fingers into the outstretched band and once more open the hand to cause the band to fly back onto the first two fingers.

Effect No. 3   Place a red band over the first and second fingers, as before. Then put a blue band on the third and fourth (see Fig. 119). Insert the right forefinger into the blue

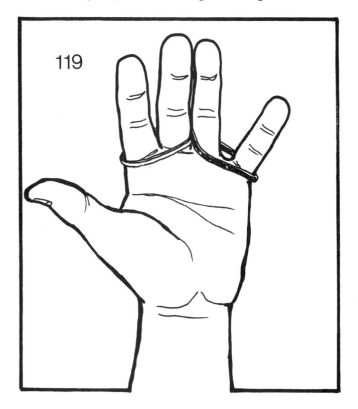

119

band and then into the red band (Fig. 120). Draw them both forward, stretching the band to enable you to insert all your bent-down fingers into them. (Fig. 121). Let the bands go as in Fig. 122. Open the hand and the bands will flip across, changing places.

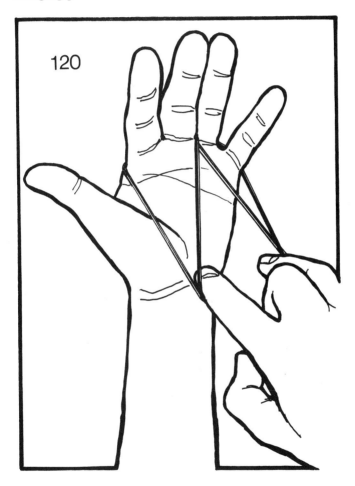

120

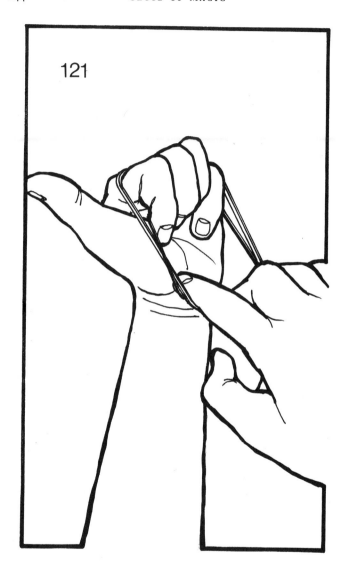

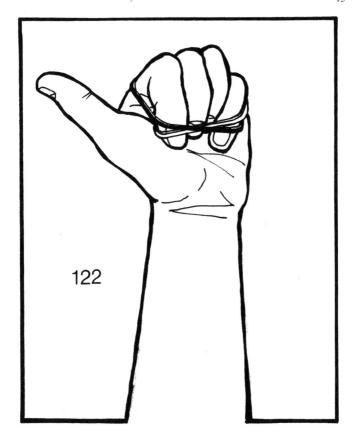

122

Effect No. 4 Insert three fingers of the right hand into the right-hand band, stretching it towards you. With right thumb assisting, insert the fingers also into the band on the left. Close the left hand and, as you do so, insert all fingers into the two bands being held stretched open by the right fingers. Take away the right hand. Open the left smartly to cause the bands to hop back to their original places.

Effect No. 5 Leave them in this position (as at end of
Effect No. 4). Take a third band and twist it round all the
left fingers, as shown in Fig. 123. This will prove to the

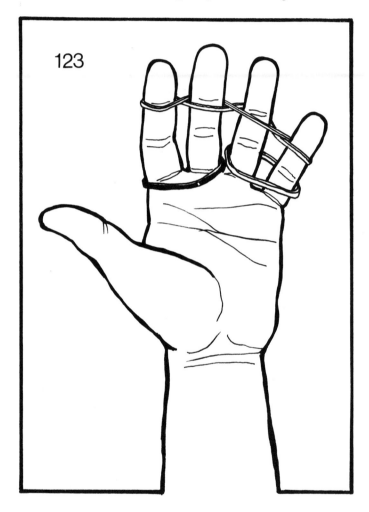

123

spectators that the bands do not in fact fly off the top of the fingers. With this band in place, repeat Effect No. 3 and, despite the restriction, the bands will still change places. Fig. 124 shows how the bands are stretched even though the

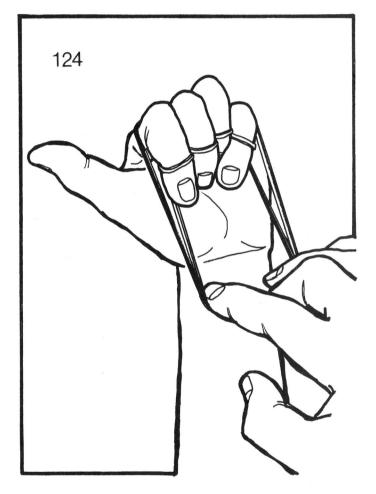

124

large band encircles the fingers. Fig. 125 shows the bands have transposed themselves after the hand is opened. NB   All the drawings are as seen by you.

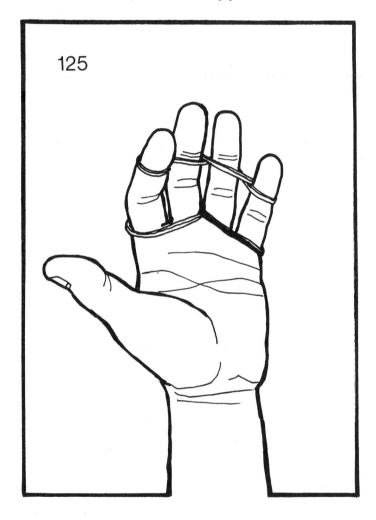

125

BANDIT

STILL on the subject of elastic bands, we can go a stage further with another trick, one, incidentally, which has baffled many magicians. It is not widely known, so it is well worth practising.

All that is needed is a solid curtain ring about an inch or slightly larger in diameter and an elastic band about 5 inches in circumference. The band is wound round the fingers of the left hand and a ring is then dropped over the second finger (Fig. 126). Although it is impossible to push it down to the bottom, because of the elastic band, you do just that! The right thumb and forefinger grasp the ring and push it down so that it seems to penetrate right through the band (see Fig. 127). Both sides of the hand are shown. Eventually the ring is removed in the same startling manner.

First of all the band is entwined round the fingers, but you must twist the band *twice* before it goes on the next finger. In the normal way, you would perhaps give only one twist to make the band encircle the fingers, but in this instance you must give a *double* twist before passing on to the next finger. Show your hand back and front at this stage. Now comes the secret move. As you pick up the ring, lower the left hand and secretly remove the second finger from the band. Hold the hand, palm to the audience with the free finger pressing against the band. The appearance is as before, i.e. all fingers are encircled. Fig. 127 is a photo taken after the second finger has been removed and is being held against the band as described. As you can see, the illusion is perfect. But Fig. 128 shows the back of the hand as it appears to you, the second finger really being free of the band.

The ring is picked up by the right forefinger and thumb and placed over the second finger and an attempt is made to force it down through the band. The spectators see

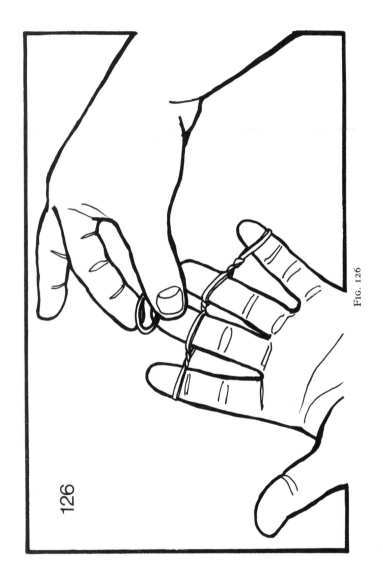

FIG. 126

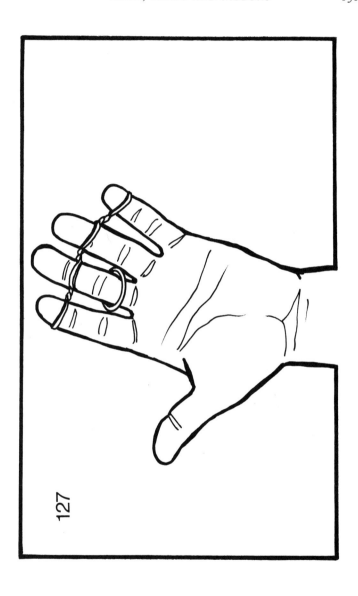

127

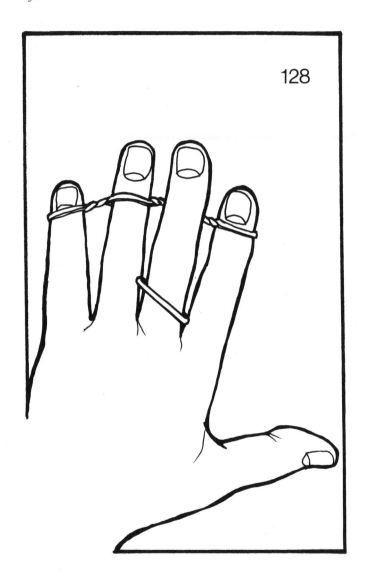

that it is impossible—but suddenly you push it right through, penetrating the band. Turn the hand over and, as you do so, bend the finger and bring it back up behind the band—no difference is apparent. Practise this reverse palm movement so that you can show both sides of the hand. Finally remove the ring in the same dramatic manner, passing this and the band for inspection.

RIBBON PENETRATION

THIS is one of the most baffling of close-up tricks. The ribbon appears to penetrate a person's finger and is immediately passed for inspection.

The special apparatus is easily made as follows: Secure a length of $\frac{1}{2}$-inch ribbon about 10 inches long; on this, thread two solid curtain rings. Now sew the ends of the ribbon together and you have an endless loop of ribbon on which is secured two rings (see Fig. 129). Pass the ribbon for

129

examination, then take it back and hold the two rings on the right thumb. Now appear to take one ring back with the left fingers—actually, it is left behind in the right hand and only the loop of ribbon is taken.

It appears to the audience that you are holding the loop of ribbon fully extended, one ring in each hand (in actual fact, of course, the two rings are in the right hand, both at one end of the loop). Now place the ribbon over someone's finger. Bring both hands together for a second and secure one of the rings in the left fingers. Then suddenly pull the ribbon smartly, at the same time releasing the loop with the left hand. Separate the rings and the ribbon straightens out in front of the finger, having apparently passed completely through it.

Conclusion

WELL! That just about winds up the book. If you have had some fun doing the various tricks, and in so doing have given your friends much pleasure, then the purpose of this book will have been achieved. Wherever you go you will always be able to divert and entertain those around you, and the knowledge gleaned from these pages will stand you in good stead from now on.

I am grateful to all those conjurors, known and unknown, from whom this material has come in some form or another. In many cases the origins of tricks, particularly of the close-up variety, are lost in obscurity and it is seldom practical to give credit for the invention of tricks unless one is certain in doing so. For this reason I have in the main refrained from mentioning such names and sources.

The subject has endless variations, and if your interest as a reader has been aroused and sustained, may I cherish the hope that you will in turn be able to pass on to the magical fraternity as a whole some stunning routine or effect which you will surely dream up sooner or later.

Glossary/Index

Hold the pack face down in the left hand with the left thumb against the outer left corner of the deck. The left forefinger is curled beneath and pressing upwards. The other three fingers are curled round the right-hand side of the pack.

The right-hand approaches with the right thumb

pressing against the inner end of the pack (nearest body). The left thumb releases the two top cards, levering them upwards, while the right thumb lifts up their bottom ends. Kept well squared up they can now be lifted off the pack to be shown as one card.

Effect, p. 9. The overall impression the trick has on the audience; what it looks like from the spectator's point of view.

Fabulous 'Paddle' Move, The, p. 91.

Face Down. When the card or cards are placed face down it means that the faces are downwards, with the patterned side or backs of the cards on top. Also **Face Up,** i.e. the cards are held with the values showing.

Fade-away Coin, p. 62.

Fake or **Feke.** See also **Gimmick.** A part of the apparatus so prepared as to make the trick possible.

Finger Palm, p. 91. An object such as a ball or coin is concealed in the hand and held by the fingers which are curled inwards towards the palm.

Flip-over Bands, p. 137.

Gimmick. A special device used in connection with a trick. More often than not its presence is unsuspected by the audience.

Glimpse. To note secretly a word in a book, or the bottom card while holding the pack face down.

Gully-gully, p. 120.

Hamburg Rope Trick, p. 42.

Impromptu Book Test, p. 34.

Indestructable String, p. 41.

It's a Knock-out, p. 32.

Key of Endor, The, p. 101.

'Knot' by Tube, p. 55.

Linking Mint, p. 101.

Living and Dead, p. 39.

Lucillus, p. 118.

Magic Wand, p. 118.

Magician's Club, p. 25.

Mark, The, p. 114.

Mechanic's Ghost, The, p. 102.

Mind Bender, p. 38.

Miscall, p. 9.

Misdirect. Temporarily to distract the spectator's attention while a secret manoeuvre or sleight takes place.

Moves. Manoeuvres executed by the conjuror to bring about the trick.

Mystery Knots, p. 133.

Newspaper Prediction, p. 34.

No Smoking, p. 109.

Pack. The complete pack of 52 cards. See also **Deck.**

Paddle Move, p. 91.

Panama Rope Trick, p. 43.

Patriotic Pots, p. 87.

Pinch of Smoke, A, p. 33.

Plop, p. 106.

Pompeii, p. 101.

Prepare. See also **Setting Up.** To arrange and set articles ready for the performance.

Principle. The basic method by which the trick is accomplished.

Props, p. 22. The term used in this book to indicate pieces of apparatus or magical equipment. From the word 'properties', i.e. stage properties.

Puzzleloop, p. 59.

Quick Four Ace, p. 17.

Rattling Good Trick, p. 78.

Reverso, p. 16.

Ribbon Penetration, p. 153.

Riffle Shuffle. The cards are divided into two piles. Hold one in each hand. Each half is riffled into the other. When the pack is finally squared up, the cards have been mixed or shuffled.

Rigoletto Brothers, p. 25.

Ring and the Spring, The, p. 54.

Ring Release, p. 110.

Safety Rip, p. 51.

Seneca, p. 118.

Setting Up, p. 66. To 'get set up' for a trick is to arrange the props in position and get them fixed ready to work the effect. Also, a **'set-up pack'** is one whose cards are arranged in a set order, as for instance in the **Spell It** trick on p. 18. See also **Prepare.**

Short Change, p. 69.

Shrinking Money, p. 62.

Shuffle. To mix the cards.

Spell It, p. 18.

Squared Up. After the cards have been dealt, counted or shuffled, they are formed into a neat stack again, i.e. 'squared up'.

Stapled Coin, p. 64.

Still Dicey, p. 100.

Stooge, Confederate, Accomplice. A person who assists you unknown to the audience.

Stretching Silk, p. 127.

Super-normal Strength, p. 31.

Switch. Secretly to exchange one object for another of a similar kind, e.g. one coin can be switched for another.

Three Little Cups, p. 118.